Adam S Johnston

The Soldier Boy's Diary Book

Memorandums of the alphabetical first lessons of Military Tactics

Adam S Johnston

The Soldier Boy's Diary Book
Memorandums of the alphabetical first lessons of Military Tactics

ISBN/EAN: 9783337087517

Printed in Europe, USA, Canada, Australia, Japan

Cover: Foto ©Andreas Hilbeck / pixelio.de

More available books at **www.hansebooks.com**

THE

Soldier Boy's Diary Book;

OR,

MEMORANDUMS

OF THE

Alphabetical First Lessons of Military Tactics.

KEPT BY

ADAM S. JOHNSTON.

From September 14, 1861, to October 2, 1864.

PITTSBURGH:
1866.

Entered according to Act of Congress, on the thirteenth day of
April, A. D. 1867,

BY ADAM S. JOHNSTON.

In the Clerk's Office of the District Court of the U
Western District of Pennsylvania

PREFACE

In taking up a book of any kind, your first glance is to see its form, or name set forth in it, from what source it originated, or who is its author.

First. The following pages have been filled up by me, Adam S. Johnston, its author and finisher, a member of Company D, Captain J. S. M'Bride, Seventy-ninth Regiment of Pa. Vols. Infantry, Colonel H. A. Hambright commanding. Gen. Negley's Brigade.

Second. The names of camps, destinations, marches and number of miles marched during 1861, 1862, 1863 and 1864, and the fiery trials, hardships and battles personally engaged in; when wounded, and in what battle; how long absent from my company and regiment, on account of wound, and my return to join them, and where at.

Third. Capture and imprisonment; while a prisoner, confined in Smith's and Pemberton's buildings in Richmond, Va., on Cary street, near the well known Libby prison and Castle Thunder, and many other places of confinement, equal to Belle Island, which would make a heart, although hard as steel, melt to know how fast many of my brother soldiers' lives were shortened and taken away by scores, yes, I would be safe in saying hundreds per day, by starvation, and want of clothing, and ill-traatment, while in the jaws and hands of the enemy in those hellish places of confinement.

Fourth. And all the comfort or consolation those fast wasting frames and sickened bodies had, was to lie down on a hard, rough plank-floor, with the soft side of a brick for a pillow on which to rest their weary heads; which had to be stolen or pried out of the walls by some of the inmate brother soldiers, or they or I would be even deprived of that privilege or comfort.

Fifth. To give you some idea of those prisons in Richmond, Va., and likewise in Danville, Va., while confined there. They consisted of a large brick building or buildings, formerly used for pressing and manufacturing tobacco by the Sunny South's inhabitants. their length being three hundred feet and twenty-four feet wide, containing three stories in height, and three hundred men in each room, without furniture of any kind, and nothing but the floor to sit or lie down on, and kept without fire all the time, even in the coldest time of frosts and winter, and inhabited by the army-bug or grey-backs, and all the filth that mortal eye could discern.

Sixth. I might fill page after page with the sufferings and hardships of the poor Union soldiers, which they endured without a murmur after the misfortune of being captured when standing up in defense of their country's rights and privileges, and then placed in those filthy and crowded prisons, which no artist can paint or human tongue describe.

Seventh. And not finished then, but time and space will not permit to go further. And now I will turn your attention to the out-starts of our camps and marches, and number of miles marched from one camp to the other, and the time of our stay in each and every camp, from the period above spoken of till my return, October 2d, 1864.

The Soldier Boy's Diary.

Sept. 14, 1861. Exchanged home and friends and all that was near and dear to me, for camp life, and left home, with a final farewell, for the seat of war. Went to the town of Buena Vista, Allegheny Co., Pa., to bid farewell to my oldest daughter and youngest son, and stayed all night at John Wood's. A march of 17 miles.

Sept. 15. Left for Monongahela City with ten members for Company D, of the 79th Pa. Vols. Infantry; arrived in the camp or fair ground in the above named place, Washington county, Pa., in time for supper, and was happily received by our captain, and after supper escorted up into town for lodging and entertainment for the night—making a march of 12 miles.

Sept. 16. Sworn into Company D by a justice of the peace of the town of Monongahela City, and afterward formed into line, and a farewell speech made to us by the Rev. J. C. Brown (of the M. E. Church) of the same city, in behalf of us as soldiers going out in defense of our country, and sacrificing home, friends and all that was near and dear to us, and bidding us a final farewell. Who was followed by Mr. M'Bride, the father of our captain, giving us a hearty welcome for choice of our captain, and then presenting him with a very nice sword, saying, "Take this, and never surrender it to those traitors against whom you have been called out to battle with, and may it not be returned till stained to the hilt, or peace once more restored to our now distracted country." With a final farewell we were marched down to the river's brink, to enter on board a fine steamboat there ready to receive us and to convey us from our friends, who escorted us to the boat, with ten thousand cheers for our welfare and safe return again. But, alas! how many of us never did return. We got to Pittsburgh the same night, took supper at the Girard House, and left for the cars on Liberty street, at 12 o'clock at night, *en route* for Lancaster; but owing to a train running off on the Chicago R. R. we were detained till morning. Making a march of 28 miles.

Sept. 17. Left Pittsburgh and got to Lancaster on the night of the 18th, about 4 o'clock in the morning; slept in the Rankin House till morning, took breakfast and then were marched up near the Pennsylvania rail road and quartered in a hook and ladder house for sixteen days, and drilled and put through the manual of arms about four hours per day during those sixteen days, being our first alphabetical lessons of military tactics. Making a march of 339 miles.

Oct. 4. Left Lancaster and got to Harrisburg the same day; drew our first tents and pitched them for the first time; drew our first blankets, stood our first sentinel beats around camp, and our first duty required. Making a march of 90 miles.

Oct. 5. Left Harrisburg and got to Pittsburgh the 7th, being one day and night *en route*, and encamped in Camp Wilkins, well known by the citizens and surrounding neighborhood as the fair ground. Making a march of 249 miles.

Oct. 17. Left Pittsburgh for Louisville, being ten days in Camp Wilkins, getting equipped and fitted out. Went on board the "Silver Wave" steamboat, and a short time after the front part of the hurricane deck gave way, letting many of our soldiers and musicians fall to the lower deck, hurting two men badly. We moved down the Ohio river three days and three nights, cheered from either shore by hundreds, and safely reached Louisville, Ky., on the 20th of October. Making a march of 625 miles.

Oct. 23. Left Louisville, having remained three days in that city and fair ground, making a march of three miles out of town and three back again, which will make six miles. Got to Camp Nevin on the 23d of October, the place where our first division commander, General Rousseau, defeated the rebels and made them skedaddle back to Horse Cave City in Kentucky. Making a march of 72 miles.

Nov. 26. Left Camp Nevin, making one month and three days in camp. Got to Camp Negley on the same day. A march of 3 miles.

Dec. 5th. Left Camp Negley, after remaining there nine days; got to Camp Hambright the same day. Making a march of 1½ miles.

Dec. 11. Left Camp Hambright, after remaining there six days. Got to Camp Wood, Baking creek, on the 11th. Making a march of 12 miles.

Dec. 16. Left Camp Wood, Baking creek, Ky., after remaining there five days, and got to Camp Woodsonville, Green river, Ky., making a march of 11 miles. Had to fall in battle-line about ten minutes after receiving order to pitch tents, and go over Green river to reinforce Col. Willich, whom the rebels had attacked; but before we reached the river Col. Willich and his small command had whipped them and driven four thousand of them back. We then got orders to return again to camp. Twelve of Col. Willich's men killed and seventeen wounded, on the 16th day of December, 1861, the day we arrived in Camp Woodsonville. Making a march of two miles to the battle-ground and two from it—4 miles.

Feb. 14, 1862. Left Camp Woodsonville, Ky., on our first march or counter-march, for two months all but two days remaining in this camp. Getting marching orders to our whole Western Army to right-about or counter-march to West Point, 20 miles down the Ohio river, below Louisville, going a march of 14 miles through mud and snow six inches deep, and encamp for the night, not having our tents with us, on account of the roads being so bad that our baggage-wagons could not reach us; so we had to make ourselves as comfortable as possible by building square pens of rails, and sleeping on the tops of these pens, to keep us out of the snow and from the frosts of winter.

Feb. 15. Got marching orders to right-about and

counter-march back over the same road again to Camp Hambright, with our whole army, making a march of 7 miles and encamping for the night.

Feb. 16. Left Camp Hambright, and marched back past our old Camp Woodsonville and on over Green river two miles, and encamped for the night, naming the camp after our Col. Hambright again. Making a march of 16 miles.

Feb. 17. Left Camp Hambright, remaining in this camp two days, and went on a march for Bowling Green. Got to Camp Water Cave, or a branch of the great Mammoth Cave, so well known to exist in Kentucky. Making a march of 22 miles.

Feb. 23. Left Water Cave Camp, remaining six days in this camp, and got to Camp Starkweather the same day, making a march of 21 miles.

Feb. 27. Left Camp Starkweather, after remaining there four days, and got to Camp Franklin the same day, making a march of 23 miles.

Feb. 28. Left Camp Franklin, and got to Cain creek, and encamped for the night, making a march of 19 miles.

March 1. Left Cain creek, after remaining there one day, and got to the Cumberland river on the same day, and encamped for the night, making a march of 15 miles.

March 2. Left the Cumberland river and got to Camp Hambright the same day, making a march of 8 miles.

March 6. Left Camp Hambright and got to Camp Andrew Johnson, two miles from Nashville, Tenn., the same day, making a march of 4 miles.

March 29. Left Camp Andrew Johnston and got to Camp Merriweather, Franklin, Tenn.—a most beautiful camp—and encamped for the night, making a march of 17 miles.

April 1. Left Camp Merriweather, and got to Camp Rutherford the same day, and encamped for the night, remaining one day in this place, making a march of 20 miles.

April 2. Left Camp Rutherford and got to Duck creek the same day, and encamped for the night, making a march of 2 miles.

April 3. Left Duck creek camp and got to Camp General Moorhead the same day, and encamped for the night, making a march of 5 miles.

May 10. Left Camp General Moorhead and came to Columbia, and got to the town of Pulaski on the same day, and encamped for the night, making a march of 11 miles.

May 13. Left Pulaski and got to Sugar creek on the same day, remaining three days in the above mentioned camp, and encamped for the night, making a march of 18 miles.

May 14. Left Sugar creek camp and got to Rogersville, four miles from the Tennessee river, and had just unslung our knapsacks, when orders came for us to fall in and go double-quick down to the Tennessee river—that the rebels had attacked our cavalry at Lamb's Landing or Ferry, Laudle Co. Our first fire or engagement with the enemy. Two men of our forces were wounded and two horses killed. The rebels were compelled to retreat from there in double-quick order—their loss unknown, as they retreated in the night. We returned to camp, making four miles to the battle-ground and four back again, in all a march of 8 miles; and having made 29 miles of a march the same day before being called into action, making a total march of 37 miles.

May 16. Left Rogersville or Lamb's Landing, remaining two days in the above mentioned camp, got within one mile of Florence, Alabama, the same day, and encamped for the night, making a march of 20 miles.

May 17. Left this camp and marched into the town of Florence, and encamped for the night, making a march of 1 mile.

May 18. Left Florence camp and marched to the Alabama line, between it and Tennessee a right-about or counter-march again for Tennessee. Slept this night in camp with my feet in Alabama and my head in Tennessee, after making a march of 20 miles.

May 19. Left the Tennessee and Alabama line, got to Lawrenceburg, Tenn., the same day, and encamped for the night at Lawrenceburg camp, making a march of 20 miles.

May 20. Left Lawrenceburg camp and got to Mount Pleasant the same day, and encamped for the night, making a march of 20 miles.

May 21. Left Camp Mount Pleasant and got back to our old camp General Moorhead, at Columbia, Tenn., making a march of 11 miles. Return of a grand scout all safe and sound, except two men lost in the battle of Lamb's Ferry, above spoken of.

May 26. Left General Moorhead camp and got to within five miles of Gillespie,' after remaining five days in the above camp, and encamped for the night, making a march of 27 miles.

May 29. Left Gillespie camp and got to a high mountain on the Fayetteville road, called Barren Point, and encamped for the night, after remaining three days in the above mentioned camp, making a march of 23 miles.

May 31. Left Barren Point camp and marched one mile east of Fayetteville, and encamped for the night at Camp Wynkoop, making a march of 19 miles.

June 2. Left Camp Wynkoop and got to Camp Haggerty, one mile south of Salem, in Franklin, Tenn., making one day in the above mentioned camp, and encamped for the night, making a march of 22 miles.

June 3. Left Camp Haggerty and marched on the Chattanooga road, encamped for the night at Cowen's Station, making a march of 21 miles.

June 4. Left Cowen's Station and marched over the Cumberland mountains to Cumberland Gap or Sweden Valley. Came upon a camp of General Adams' rebel cavalry, seven thousand in number, who stood us a fight, being the second engagement that we were personally engaged in. Three fires from our batteries put them to flight; and in following up their retreat we lost two men out of Col. Haggerty's regiment of Kentucky cavalry. Our forces captured a first-rate cooked dinner, just ready to be sit down to eat; and corn, leather and ammunition of all kinds, haversacks made out of every sort of material, women's carpet-sacks and clothes, even down to babies' frocks, that these scoundrels had stolen from the Union families of the valley they had passed through—all of which fell into our hands; and those hellish fiends had to flee from to save capturing of themselves and their whole army, losing many of their men killed and wounded by our forces, and a number of prisoners falling into our hands. After dinner we encamped for the night on their camp or battle-ground, making a march of 15 miles.

June 5. Left Sweden Cove Valley camp and marched through Jaspertown on the Chattanooga road, and encamped in camp meeting barracks, used for holding camp meetings in, nicely fitted up for that purpose, and called Camp Mellinger, making a march of 15 miles.

June 6. Left Camp Mellinger and arrived 12½ miles this side of Chattanooga, and encamped for the night at Camp Sliver, making a march of 27 miles.

June 7. Left Camp Sliver and arrived at Camp Haste, 12½ miles. At 2 o'clock, got orders to fall in again for fight. We marched about one mile, feeling our way cautiously as we went, understanding that fifteen thousand rebels had crossed the Tennessee river and were moving on us, between the river and town, in haste. There were two companies of the 79th Pa. Inf. detailed and sent down the river in front of Chattanooga, to advance slowly and cautiously to feel the enemy; while a force of cavalry was sent around to come up the river and advance until they would meet, if not fired upon. The rest of our army, with six pieces of artillery, passing down the river on the right, about one mile and a quarter from the river, to the centre, and our brave commander, General Negley, at the head of our forces, gave us the order to left face and advance toward the river and town. On we went to the top of a high hill or mountain in sight of the town, which surprised the rebels in their forts and town to see the Yankees in sight; so the orders, "Lie down, infantry, flat to the ground, and be ready to support your batteries," was no sooner given than it was obeyed. We could see the rebs coming out of their forts and pits like bees out of a soap, and turning their artillery on us; so feeling that our cavalry and infantry might meet, and hearing they were across the river, might fire on each other when meeting, four men were detailed off the head of each company, to be sent down to the river as skirmishers, to report to them, and then return to the hill again. As I was one of the front files, it so happened to be my lot to go, and on reaching the river the rebs opened fire on us from the other side, killing two men and wounding several of our force. At three o'clock we opened our batteries on them and their town, shelling them hard, and causing them to silence their guns, only four shots of theirs reaching us. We shelled the town until four in the evening, causing them all to move out of the town and call for reinforcements from the Gap, which was all we wanted, to draw them out with this feint attack, so that our army might go in, which it did without being interrupted, the rebs having evacuated the place. So we returned back to camp for the night, making a march of 14 miles.

June 8. Left Camp Haste, having fulfilled our mission, and after shelling the town of Chattanooga this morning again about three hours, we took up march right-about or counter-marched back again to our old camp Sliver, making a march of 12½ miles.

June 9. Left Sliver on our return and encamped for the night on the M'Minnville road at Big Creek camp, making a march of 27 miles.

June 10. Left Big Creek camp and marched on the Altamont road to Camp Nell and encamped for the night, making a march of 21 miles.

June 11. Left Camp Nell and arrived at Manchester the same night, and encamped, making a march of 25 miles.

June 12. Left Manchester camp and arrived at Shelbyville, and encamped for the night at Camp Cooper, making a march of 25 miles.

July 8. Left Camp Cooper, and arrived the same day at Wartrace, remaining in the above mentioned camp twenty-six days, without moving. Encamped for the night in Wartrace, guarding commissary or station all night; making a march of 8 miles.

July 9. Left Wartrace and arrived at Duck river the same day as guard for rail road bridges and fortifications there, and encamped for the night at Duck river bridge camp, making a march of 5 miles.

July 14. Left Camp Duck river and arrived the same day at Tullahoma and encamped for the night. making a march of 9 miles.

July 25. Left Tullahoma and marched to Manchester fair grounds, Coffee county, Tenn., and encamped for the night, making a march of 11 miles.

Aug. 10. Left Manchester camp and arrived at Tullahoma the same day, and encamped for the night, making a march of 12 miles.

Aug. 11. Left Tullahoma camp and arrived at Nashville the same day, and encamped for the night, making a march of 70 miles.

Aug. 12. Left Nashville camp and moved four miles out of town to camp, and was rallied the same day and slept all night on our arms, with sixty rounds of cartridges, in the town of Nashville, Tenn., making a march of four miles and four back again, making 8 miles.

Aug. 13. Left camp again and slept all night on our arms in Nashville, and encamped or changed camp the same day on College Hill, 1½ miles out of town, making a march of 2½ miles.

Aug. 16. Left Camp College Hill, or was rallied and sent to Gallatin, Summer county, Tenn., and slept on our arms all night, and the next morning our company was sent out to ascertain where company K, of the 79th Pa. Inf. was, as they were put on out-post picket in the night and could not be found in the morning. We found them on the Gallatin road, one mile from town; in the mean time orders came to right-about and march to camp again. On arriving there, orders had come to the regiment to right-about and march to College Hill again, leaving Co. D behind. So we lay over until the next day, and a train of cars came for us and we returned again to camp, making a march of 23 miles.

Aug. 17. Returned to camp, making a march of 13 miles, remaining in this camp four days.

Aug. 21. Left Camp College Hill on a rally from Nashville to the junction of the L. R. & G. rail road and returned to Nashville the same day, and was ordered right back the same night, making a march of 30 miles.

Aug. 22. Left as an escort for General Nelson to Franklin, Tenn., from camp at the junction of the L. R. & G. rail road, and encamped at Tire Spring for the night, making a march of 12 miles.

Aug. 23. Left Tire Spring camp and arrived at Drake's mill, Franklin, the same day, and encamped for the night, having fulfilled our escort, making a march of 22 miles.

Aug. 24. Left Drake's mill camp and arrived the same day in Franklin, and encamped for the night, making a march of 2 miles.

Aug. 25. Left Franklin camp and arrived at the tunnel of the Louisville & Nashville R. R. the same day, and encamped for the night, making a march of 22 miles.

Aug. 26. Left the Tunnel camp and arrived at Gallatin on the same day, driving General Morgan and his forces out of the above named town, killing one of the rebel pickets because he would not halt when ordered by one of our number, and took possession of the town for the night, making a march of 7 miles.

Aug. 27. Left Gallatin and returned to our old camp on College Hill, Nashville, making another grand circle the same day, a march of 26 miles.

Aug. 28. Left Camp College Hill on the night of the 27th on a rally of double-quick for Columbia. Lay there all night and the 28th in battle line, making a march of 45 miles.

Aug. 29. Left Columbia camp, the half of our regiment coming from Pulaski, 35 miles of a march, and returned to camp the same day, and encamped for the night, making another march this same day of 45 miles.

Sept. 4. Left Camp College Hill again and arrived at Goodlettsville on the 5th and took breakfast, making a march of 12 miles.

Sept. 5. Left Goodlettsville and arrived at Tire Spring camp, making the third time in this camp and our third march and counter-march over this ground, and encamped for the night, making a march of 9½ miles.

Sept. 6. Left Camp Tire Spring and arrived the same day at Franklin and encamped for the night, making a march of 22 miles.

Sept. 7. Left Franklin camp, and arrived the same day at Bowling Green, encamping for the night, making a march of 21 miles.

Sept. 8. Left Bowling Green camp and changed camp near Big Barren river the same day, and encamped for the night, making a march of 3 miles.

Sept. 12. Left Big Barren River camp and changed camp to the centre of Bowling Green the same day, remaining four days in the above mentioned camp, making a march of 1½ miles.

Sept. 16. Left Bowling Green camp and got to the

Great Cave Spring the same day, and encamped for the night, making a march of 4 miles.

Sept. 17. Left the Great Cave Spring camp and arrived the same day at Robin Hood, near the Dripping Springs, making a march of 18 miles.

Sept. 18. Left Dripping Springs camp and arrived at Deaumont Knob the same day, and encamped for the night, making a march of 18 miles.

Sept. 19. Left Deaumont Knob camp and arrived at Bell's Knob the same day, and encamped for the night, making a march of 5 miles. Was rallied and fell into line of battle, and had a skirmish with the enemy, losing four men on our side, but we succeeded in routing them the same day.

Sept. 20. Left Bell's Knob camp and marched to Glasgow, Union county, Tenn., the same day, and encamped for the night, making a march of 24 miles.

Sept. 21. Left Glasgow camp and arrived at Green river the same day, and fatigued and tired, laid down for the night in camp, making a march of 25 miles. On arriving in this camp the Green river bridge, which is thrown across that stream, with four piers, one hundred and fifty five feet from low-water mark, was on fire and falling, having been fired by the rebels on their retreat while we were following them up, and all the pontoon flats of a bridge thrown across said stream burned to the water's edge, to save their retreat.

Sept. 22. Left Green river camp and marched to Nolin the same day, making a march of 22 miles.

Sept. 23. Left Nolin camp and marched to Mulgrove Valley the same day, and encamped for the night, making a march of 25 miles.

Sept. 26. Left Nolin camp and marched to Louisville, Ky., on the morning of the 27th, and encamped in the town for three days, to rest and recruit and get four months' pay, and draw clothing, making a march of 31 miles. Being the second time we encamped in Louisville.

Oct. 1. Left Louisville camp and marched to South Fork, and encamped for the night, making a march of 20 miles.

Oct. 2. Left South Fork camp, marched to Taylorsville, and went three miles out on picket the same night, making a march of 23 miles.

Oct. 4. Left Taylorsville camp, remaining the 3d on picket and marched the 4th to Bloomington, and encamped for the night, making a march of 10 miles.

Oct. 6. Left Bloomington and marched over Chaplin creek on the hill the same day, having remained in the above mentioned camp two days, and encamped for the night, making a march of 11 miles.

Oct. 7. Left Chaplin creek camp and marched to McMinnville, Ky., the same day, and encamped for the night, making a march of 15 miles.

Oct. 8. Left McMinnville camp in the morning, the colonel telling us, "Boys, you have longed to meet the enemy on the battle-field, and you will have a chance to-day, or do without water, as the enemy holds the spring that we will have to encamp at." The shout went up from every son of Uncle Sam's family, "A fight and water we will have." The cannons were already booming, and had been all night, so at fifteen minutes past two o'clock we became engaged, and in one hour and three-quarters we lost two hundred and eleven men out of our regiment (the 79th Pa. Vol. Infantry). We went into the fight with forty-three men in our company (D) and came out with eighteen, having had twenty-five wounded and killed; two killed dead and two dying the next day. I myself was unfortunate enough to be shot through the left leg, about two inches below the knee, the ball glancing off the bone and passing through and out at the fleshy part or calf of the leg, injuring the muscle so that I was unfit for fight, and was sent to the rear after the fifteenth fire. This is my first and last wound received in the battle of Chaplin Hill or Chaplin Heights, so called, and fought on the 8th day of October, 1862, in Boyle county, Ky. Making a march of 8 miles.

Oct. 9. Was hauled from off the battle-ground in an ambulance wagon at half past two in the morning, for fear of the enemy opening fire on our hospital or old house in which we remained all night from the day of the fight; having our batteries planted close by, if another engagement would ensue, they would draw the enemy's fire on our building. So we, four in number, were hauled five miles this morning to Antioch church, Boyle county, and thrown out in a pile like wood, for they had been removing wounded off the battle-ground all night until the church was perfectly filled, and under every shade tree nigh at hand. I rolled over and over, as I was so disabled that I could not walk, until I got to a fence, and with loss of blood and pain and fatigue, became sleepy in a short time after; being left in this condition, I went to sleep and slept until after the sun was up, and on awaking I found myself completely tight against the above mentioned fence. on account of another wounded soldier dying while I was asleep, with his feet tight down the hill against me and his head up the hill, the ground being somewhat rolling. I called to a citizen close by, that had come to see the wounded soldiers, to come to me and remove the dead man, that I might help myself up by the fence. He removed the person, and throwed a blanket over the body to protect it until better attended to. I lay for six days out under a white oak tree, with my wound dressed once. Making a march of 5 miles.

Oct. 15. Left or was taken from Antioch church to Perryville to a hospital fitted up for our reception. The first time away from my regiment and company from the time I left for the seat of war, or the first roll-call missed, or stacking of arms, or march missed for over a year; and was well cared for in this hospital by the surgeon in charge of us wounded Union soldiers. We were well supplied with food calculated to suit our weak and delicate appetites, from the Union citizens, women and men, of Boyle county, and got along as well as could be expected for the time of our stay in this hospital, remaining eight days in it. Making a march of 6 miles.

Oct. 23. Left Perryville. Orders came for us to be removed to Lebanon hospital; so the same day we were shipped aboard our army wagon train and arrived in Lebanon about 4 o'clock in the evening, and were happily received and met by our General Starkweather, who came to see us for the first time from the fight, and sympathized with us for our wounds, and thanked us kindly for our good behavior in the battle. This will show that we remained in the hospital above mentioned eight days. and in this one four days. Making a march of 20 miles.

Oct. 27. Left Lebanon hospital, or was ordered to be sent to Louisville No. 12 hospital, and arrived there the same evening, and was conveyed to the hospital and well cared for. Making a march of 84 miles.

Nov. 6. Left Louisville, and was sent by orders to New Albany, Indiana, hospital No. 6, and a nice place too and well cared for, remaining nine days in this hospital, and making a march of 4 miles.

Jan. 9, 1863. Left Indiana hospital No. 6 and came to Louisville Exchange barracks the same day a stay of two months and three days in this hospital making a march of 4 miles.

Jan. 10. Changed across the street to No. 1 barracks, the barracks being moved to this place the evening previous, remaining two days in these barracks making a march of ¼ mile.

Jan. 12. Left Louisville barracks and came to Portland the same day, making a march of 3 miles.

Jan. 13. Entered on board the steamer "Lady Franklin," detailed for guard down the Ohio river and around up the Cumberland river, with a fleet of twenty-seven steamboats and two gunboats, carrying provisions up to Nashville, and came to Leavenworth. A march of 60 miles.

Jan. 14. Passed down the Ohio river safely and

arrived at Evansville at 12 o'clock at night, making a march of 140 miless.

Jan. 15. Passed safely down the Ohio river to the mouth of Cumberland river at Smithland. A march of 140 miles.

Jan. 16. Passed up the Cumberland river all safe, and arrived at Fort Donelson the same day, making a march of 85 miles.

Jan. 17. Moved slowly and cautiously, feeling our way up the Cumberland river, arriving at Clarksville in the afternoon, capturing one rebel major and horse on the right of the river opposite the said town, and shortly afterward saw some rebel cavalry skulking in sight on the same side of the river above spoken of, when we ran four batteries of our forces down to the river out of Clarksville, and opened upon them, making them skedaddle. Making a march of 35 miles.

Jan. 18. Moved up the Cumberland river from Clarksville to the shoals, where three of our boats were captured two weeks before, and all the negroes who were on board shot and the whites paroled, and the boats fired and burned. We passed safely on up until our two last boats were about over the shoals first spoken of, and the "Mary Franklin" and "Woodside" were fired into, wounding one colonel, but we escaped being captured.

Jan. 19. Came to Nashville, our place of destination, at 12 o'clock and put up in the rebel Zollicoffer's house, used as barracks by our forces, making a march of 60 miles.

Jan. 20. Left Nashville on foot to join my company and regiment again. Came twenty-three miles through rain, and the roads being very muddy, we encamped for the night in a cedar house, used by our videttes or dispatch carriers; a march of 23 miles.

Jan. 21. Came seven miles to Murfreesboro', Tenn., and joined my company and regiment again, having been absent from my command on account of my wound four months all but ten days, making a march of 7 miles.

March 9. Went on a scout from Murfreesboro' with our whole division, marched 5 miles.

March 10. Marched 8 miles and encamped for the night.

March 11. Lay over in camp.

March 12. Went out on a scout three miles from camp. Twenty-eight rebel cavalry driving in our pickets, we fell into battle-line, but the rebels seeing our force skedaddled, and we returned again to camp the same day, making a march of 3 miles.

March 13. Lay over in camp all day on the Eagleville pike.

March 14. Returned to camp at Murfreesboro', having fulfilled our scout, remaining in this camp four days. A march of 16 miles.

March 18. Changed camp and moved two miles to a new camp south of the town, making a march of 2 miles.

March 20. Was rallied to march double-quick to reinforce Col. Hall at Milton, Tenn., and went out on the same day, having remained two days in this camp, making a march of 15 miles.

March 21. Returned from Milton battle-ground, Col. Hall having whipped the enemy before we reached him or his forces, and leaving many of the rebels wounded and dead on the ground, making a march of 15 miles.

March 26. Went on picket out on the field where Jeff. Davis made a speech to his men, 2½ miles from Murfreesboro' camp, making a march of 5 miles.

April 1. Went on picket on the Manchester pike four miles, making five days rest in camp there, and returned the next day to camp, making a march of 8 miles.

April 20. Started again from Murfreesboro' camp on a scout and arrived at Readyville, and encamped for the night two miles south of Fort Transit, making a march of 12 miles. Remained eighteen days in this camp without moving.

April 21. Left Fort Transit and arrived at Woodbury, eight miles from this place, and was ordered fourteen miles further on the same day, and encamped for the night, making in all this day a march of 22 miles.

April 22. Left Camp Woodbury and arrived the same day at a place called Small-pox camp, having received its name from the fact that at this place the inhabitants never were clear of this fearful disease. Encamped for the night, making a march this day of 17 miles.

April 23. Left Small-pox camp and arrived at Liberty, driving out the rebel General Breckinridge and all his forces, causing them to flee in all directions, and leave their camp and camp equipment behind, including a variety of almost everything you can speak of. The headquarters of General Breckinridge were set on fire by our cavalry after entering the town, and by the time the infantry got in sight were burned to the ground. The inhabitants of the town seeing they were caught for the first time by our army, began to clear their houses of furniture and contents, carrying out their hardware and throwing their brittleware out of the windows, through the excitement that the town was to be burned down ere we would leave, in retaliation for some horrible murders committed on the soldiers of the Union army by those hellish fiends of their so-called Confederacy. After searching or scouting the town, it was ascertained that there was a large steam mill, filled to the brim with wheat, flour and corn, and on entering the mill we found hidden in a pile of bran a quantity of their ammunition, having been made or manufactured at Atlanta, Georgia. It was covered up by bran being thrown over it. We were ordered to remove it to our train, together with all the flour and wheat. It was no sooner said than done; then a match was applied to the mill, and soon nothing could be seen but a pile of coals and ruins. After firing several other buildings that they used for places of concealment of this kind, we moved to camp at Smith's Fork, DeKalb county, Tenn., the same day, and encamped for the night, making a march of 20 miles.

April 24. Lay over in camp at Smith's Fork all this day quiet and unmolested.

April 25. Detailed to go out as skirmishers, and to support some batteries.

April 26. All quiet in camp at Smith's Fork.

April 27. Report of two thousand rebels in battle line on Snow Hill in the rear of Liberty, Tenn. Hearing this we were reinforced by Col. Hall and fell into battle-line and remained so for the night.

April 28. All quiet in camp to-day, only some little foraging for ducks, chickens, pigs, &c., so that the sons of Uncle Sam's family enjoyed themselves well on this day.

April 29. Left camp at Smith's Fork, DeKalb Co., Tenn., and marched five miles from this camp to Orbenstown, bringing with us many of the Union families of this county, whose whitened locks and old age, wealth and respectable appearance would make a heart, although it was as hard as stone, melt to look upon them, as they were compelled to leave their birth-place, and all that was near and dear to them, and flee from them to our protection and safety, to escape the jaws and clutches of those traitors of so desperate a character, in their old age, and robbed of their sweet homes and everything, in all probability for ever and ever, by those notorious scoundrel secesh or rebel traitors, as you or any other one may see proper to term them—for no hand can write, or artist paint, or tongue tell, the sufferings of the Union families in the Southern States, that fall into the jaws of those hellish fiends. You will please excuse me for setting forth these hard spelled words, for I can not help it, when thinking of the sufferings of our poor Union soldiers and many Union families. So our march was continued this same day to Milton battle-ground, a march of 16 miles.

April 30. Left Camp Milton battle-ground and took up our march for our old camp Murfreesboro', and arrived safe and sound in camp, having fulfilled our mission of another grand scout, making a march of 14 miles.

May 1. Went to Murfreesboro' on a visit from camp, as we were resting in camp on this day from the fatigue of our scout; being two miles to town and two back again, making 4 miles. Gave up our Sibley tents and set up our dog or shelter tents for the first time, and have a fine berth. A clear day, very warm and dry, and all quiet in camp.

The following table will give you the names of the towns traveled through up to this time in the States of Kentucky, Tennessee and Alabama:

KENTUCKY.	TENNESSEE.	ALABAMA.
Louisville,	Mitchelsville,	Rogersville,
Elizabethtown,	Springhill,	Florence,
Mumfordsville,	Nashville,	Lawrenceburg,
Woodsonville,	Franklin,	Mount Pleasant,
Horse Cave,	Columbia,	Fayetteville.
Cave City,	Linnville,	
Bowling Green,	Pulaski,	
Franklin,	Winchester.	
Brunettstown,	Salem,	
Fishersville,	Jasper,	
Taylorsville,	Chattanooga, on	
Bloomfield,	the line of Ga.,	
Chaplin,	Ala. and Tenn.,	
Maxville,	Watrace,	
Perryville, battle,	Altamont,	
Lebanon,	Manchester,	
Louisville,	Shelbyville,	
Nolinville,	Tullahoma,	
Lavern,	Smithland,	
New Albany, Ind.	Nashville,	
Louisville,	Lavern,	
Clarksville,	Murfreesboro', battle 30 Dec., '61.	

} A counter-march into this State.

It is unnecessary for me to set forth the number of miles between the towns mentioned above, as it can be found carried out in the preceding pages of this book I will now call your attention to a few of our foraging and picket marches, and number of miles marched on those occasions.

Jan. 5, 1863. Went on picket on the gunboat "Tuscumbia" at New Albany, a march of 2 miles.

Jan. 6. Returned again to camp, having been relieved by a new guard, and arrived in camp safe at 10 o'clock of said day, making a march of 2 miles.

Jan. 16. Went on picket or forage near Murfreesboro', making a march of 20 miles.

Jan. 17. Returned, being relieved, all safe to camp, making a march of 20 miles.

Feb. 18. Went on a forage, captured six rebel prisoners and fetched them into our camp the same day, making a march of 13 miles.

Feb. 19. Returned to camp, being relieved by another regiment, all safe, and encamped for the night, making a march of 13 miles.

So as this ends the pickets up to this time, I refer you now to every day in the year from the 2d of May, 1863, and its occurrences, marches, number of miles marched from that time until my capture, imprisonment and release, during the above mentioned year and 1864, until my return home—and many other occurrences during this time which I deem worthy of note, and which I will present to you who may think it worth while to turn a leaf further on.

May 2. Supernumerary and detailed to clean off the parade-ground. Clear all day until in the evening; looks for rain. Nothing new occurred in camp to-day.

May 3. Washed my clothes before guard-mounting. Guard at 9 o'clock in the morning of this same day, in the same Camp Drake, Murfreesboro'.

May 4. On guard in this same camp to-day, and a nice clear day; our Colonel, H. A. Hambright, having been absent from his command on a visit home, returns back to camp again from Lancaster, Penn., this same day.

May 5. Came off guard, having been relieved for forty-eight hours. Looks wet and is raining at 9 o'clock of this day. Got two miniatures sent to me from Wesley Richey and wife, from the State of Indiana.

May 6. Lying all day in this same camp. All quiet, wet and very cold. Col. Hambright drilled the regiment on dress-parade in the morning, and gave us the Lancaster compliments sent to us by the patriotic sons and daughters of Lancaster county and city, assuring us, that we did not know the name we bore in the above city and county, nor could he express their feelings toward us for our good behavior, and inquiring after us. He said he would just state to us, that he could have brought us ten thousand dollars with him from that county and city for our welfare and comfort, if he would have done it, but he reminded those kind friends and inhabitants that we had been paid off by our old Uncle, and had plenty to make us comfortable and happy. Farewell.

May 7. Wet and cold. Had to lay in bed all day to keep warm; rained hard all night.

May 8. In the morning cloudy and cold; looks for rain; I am out on picket with the regiment on the Bradysville pike, station No. 1; reserve two miles off; a march of 2 miles.

May 9. Returned from picket, having been relieved. Two miles of a march back to camp, all safe and sound, and had dress-parade this same day in camp; a march of 2 miles.

May 10. Sunday, and a nice warm day; nothing new in camp; had brigade dress-parade in the evening; all quiet in camp on this day.

May 11. In Camp Drake. Washed my clothes. Richmond reported taken, but in the evening found out not to be so; had dress-parade in the evening of the same day; all quiet in camp, nothing new of importance having occurred.

May 12. In Camp Drake; a fine, clear, warm morning; regimental drill in the morning; detailed in the evening to carry water for our company cooks, as it was mine and Thomas Jester's day by rotation.

May 13. A fine clear day and very warm; drilled in the morning and was reviewed in the evening. David Johnston and Cornelius Clifford, from Indiana, paid me a visit; nothing new occurred in camp.

May 14. A very wet morning. Our Lieut. Col. Miles got his leg broken below the knee, by his horse stumbling and falling; he had visited the 77th Penna. regiment, and it was on his return to our camp that he met with this accident. I carried coffee out to No. 3

station and No. 1 post in the evening, making a march there and back again of 4 miles.

May 15. A fine warm morning; took coffee out to No. 3 station and No. 1 post, making a march out and back again of 4 miles.

May 16. A fine morning; drilled until breakfast time, and then reported to the Adjutant, fully armed and equipped, to go outside the picket line to cut cedar brush to make summer shades for our officers; regimental drill in the evening; making a march outside of our picket line of 6 miles.

May 17. On camp guard this morning; a very pleasant day, cold at night, and nothing of importance occurring in camp on this day.

May 18. Came off camp guard, having been relieved; a fine warm morning; sent our dress and overcoats to Nashville.

May 19. A fine warm day; went on a visit to see David Johnston and Cornelius Clifford and others of the 42d Ind. regiment; all quiet in camp this day; making a march of 4 miles.

May 20. A nice warm day, and am on water committee for cooking and detailed to help clean streets; orders came to be ready to march at a moment's warning; took tea out to our men on picket on the Bradysville pike, making a march there and back again of 5 miles.

May 21. A warm, nice day; took coffee out to our men on picket on the Bradysville pike to No. 2 station; our videttes were fired on by the rebels in the night, who then skedaddled; all quiet in the morning; so I returned again to camp, going and coming making a march of 5 miles.

May 22. A fine warm morning; a detail out of our regiment to fence in a brigade grave-yard at Murfreesboro', or one mile south of it.

May 23. A fine warm, clear day; detailed for camp guard.

May 24. Sunday. Came off guard, having been relieved, at 9 o'clock; went through monthly inspection.

May 25. A fine warm dry morning; sick and had to go to the doctor; in the evening dress parade; all quiet in camp on this day.

May 26. A very fine day. On out-post picket on the Bradysville pike, No. 1 station, No. 1 post; all quiet at sundown; the Assistant Adjutant General from headquarters came out to inspect our line of pickets this evening; a march of 4 miles.

May 27. Returned off picket, being relieved, after being twenty-four hours on post. Presentation of a nice sword to our Colonel, H. A. Hambright, by the members of the 79th regiment of Pa. Vol. Inf. in the evening. Making a march of 4 miles.

May 28. A fine morning; drilled two hours and a half; marching orders came, to be ready at a moment's warning; in the evening brigade drill, Generals Thomas, Rousseau, Rosencrans and others present on the ground; a march of 6 miles.

May 29. A fine cool morning; rained pretty much all night, cleared up at 12 o'clock, and had dress parade in the evening.

May 30. Rained all night, and a wet morning; drilled before breakfast, and was run in by a hard shower of rain.

May 31. Sunday. A nice morning, looks for rain; very sick with pains in my head and stomach; went to Rousseau's headquarters to preaching, but it being over, Mr. Craven and I returned to our quarters. So ends another month.

June 1. A warm and dry day. General Rosencrans had grand review of all his divisions, going to the field at 9½ o'clock and coming into camp again at 2 o'clock in the afternoon, making a march of 5 miles.

June 2. Went on camp guard and was on water committee; a very wet morning; had dress parade in the evening; nothing new occurred in camp on this day.

June 3. Rained all night but cleared up in the morning, fine growing weather; all quiet at 12 o'clock this day.

June 4. Rallied in the morning, fell into battle-line, but all became quiet again. Had inspection and a report of the strength of the camp or all fit for duty. Drew eight days' rations, to put five days' in knapsacks and three days' in haversacks; drew them at 12 o'clock of this night, and then laid down and slept until 7 o'clock, still in camp and all quiet.

June 5. Last night heavy cannonading on the Shelbyville pike. This morning general orders came to every camp, that the execution of a man by the name of William A. Selkirk was to take place in our camp at 12 o'clock to-day; the whole army gathered to the spot where the scaffold was erected. There was not one tree in sight of this place, but was full on every limb from top to bottom, and an area of miles around was covered with one mass of people to witness the scene. At 1 o'clock you could see two regiments moving from the Murfreesboro' prison, slowly followed by a spring-wagon and four nice cream-colored horses, ornamented with ribbons of red, white and blue, with the criminal seated on his coffin, and the man that consulted him before and on this solemn occasion was seated with the hangman in front of his coffin in the same wagon, the driver of the team still in front of them in the wagon, and in the rear of it the only son and friends of the murdered man, and then a heavy escort followed. They all came along slowly and solemnly to the spot, and driving through and under the scaffold, with the rope adjusted to it to receive its victim, there was a final halt. Then you could see a fine looking and stout built man seated on the coffin soon to receive his mortal remains after being ushered into eternity. An awful death to die. It appeared by his capture and trial, that on or about the 1st of March this year this man and two others (of which you will see further on in these pages.) went to the house of Adam Weaver, of Williamson county, Tenn., and did willfully beat him with clubs, and sticks, and stones, and brickbats, and with knives cut him and scarred and tortured him as long as life seemed visible, and then took a knife, and pulling his tongue out as far as possible cut it off, throwing it from them, and then taking his money, left this man dead, wallowing in blood. He was afterward captured and brought to justice for this horrible crime in the presence of thousands of Union soldiers, and his God to whom he had to give an account—he being a rebel and traitor to his fellow man and country. At six minutes past 2 o'clock the trap door was unlatched from under him, leaving him hang for twenty-six minutes without a struggle. The doctors pronounced him dead, and he was cut down and placed in his coffin and removed to the place of interment promised to all of us, saying, "From dust thou came and unto dust shalt thou return again." So ends the murderer's doom on this day, the 5th of June, 1863, in Camp Drake, Tennessee.

June 6. A warm, nice day; went to Murfreesboro' on a detail to load government grub, making a march in and out to camp of 3 miles.

June 7. Sunday. A warm, nice day, and a merry day among the soldiers, after being paid off four months' pay.

June 8. A fine warm morning; detailed for camp guard; inspection by company, regiment and brigade; all quiet in camp this day.

June 9. A fine warm day; came off camp guard having been relieved. Three men of the 78th Ind. arrested for mutiny. In the evening regimental and brigade drill; all quiet in camp this evening.

June 10. A fine day; all quiet in camp; had regimental drill in the evening; saw some of the Potomac army that were transferred to our army—the 36th and 78th Ohio Reg., and many others unknown to me.

June 11. A fine warm day; all quiet in camp, and had dress parade at 5 o'clock in the evening.

June 12. A fine warm day; on the reserve to support two Kentucky batteries on the Manchester pike, standing picket—a most beautiful place; a march from camp and back of 5 miles.

June 13. A warm, nice day; came off reserve picket on the Manchester pike, being relieved, making a march to camp of 5 miles.

June 14. Sunday. A fine, warm day, and all quiet in camp, and had dress parade in the evening; a very heavy rain, continuing all night.

June 15. A fine morning; inspection at 10½ o'clock by company, and division review at 2½ o'clock; fell in battle-line—Rousseau's whole division, General Negley's brigade.

June 16. A fine day; detailed to help Wm. Graham of our company to fill up water in barrels to be hauled for cooking with. Washed my clothes; formed a battle-line at 2½ o'clock, and came off at sundown.

June 17. A fine warm day; going to have division drill at 2½ o'clock to fall in battle-line. This evening on camp guard.

June 18. A fine warm day; came off camp guard, having been relieved on this day at 25 minutes past 12. Two more men, partners in the brutal murder of Adam Weaver with the former man Selkirk, were hung both at one time, on the same scaffold that Selkirk received his doom on the 5th of this month. The wretched victims were cut down, after receiving a murderer's doom, having hung by the neck until dead. May every one that reads these pages take warning before it is too late.

June 19. A fine warm day and all quiet in camp: regimental drill in the evening.

June 20. A fine warm day. At 10½ o'clock we fell into line and formed three sides of a square at open order, double division, to see David Leisure, of Col. Bushe's 4th Ind. Battery, shot dead for desertion from our army in the face of the enemy, at or near Smith's Fork camp, near Liberty, DeKalb county, Tenn., on the 24th of March, 1863. He was captured on the 28th of the same month by our cavalry, brought back under guard to Murfreesboro', and tried and sentenced to be shot on this day, in the presence of the whole army, so that they might take warning before it was too late. At a quarter before 12 o'clock he was shot dead on his coffin, and fell off on the left side of it, being pierced by six balls, which entered his heart, twelve guns having been fired at him. So ends a traitor's or deserter's doom.

June 21. A fine warm day; took a walk, it being Sunday and off duty in camp. All quiet to-day.

June 22. A fine day, and on guard in Camp Drake, Murfreesboro'. Have marching orders at 7 o'clock in the morning for Dixey's land or rebeldom; all quiet this evening in camp.

June 23. Left Murfreesboro' camp on our march through the land of Dixey, at 11 o'clock. Commenced skirmishing on the Shelbyville pike and continued up till night, and then heavy cannonading on the Manchester pike. Drove the rebels some seven miles. It had rained hard all day, and being tired, we encamped for the night. It was company D's lot to stand out on picket in sight of the enemy this night, which was one of the wettest nights I ever saw, and will be remembered by every soldier who stood facing the enemy on a depending battle. Making a march of 11 miles.

June 24. Lay in Camp Hoover's Gap all day until in the evening. Fighting going on all day in front of us. We lost fifteen men killed out of the Ohio troops, and many were wounded and sent to the rear. Lay on picket all night. At night all became quiet again.

June 25. Left Hoover's Gap camp, having been ordered to the front. We soon came to the place of attack, to let other troops fall back or relieve them. When we got in sight of the enemy they opened fire upon us, and we returned the compliment, silencing their batteries for the night. So we lay all night again on picket in sight of the enemy. A march of 5 miles.

June 26. Left the camp called Hoover's Gap or battle-ground to go out on picket or as skirmishers, and skirmished all day until 11 o'clock, when we were ordered to make a charge on their battle-line, and made them just light out, with us getting eight men wounded out of the 79th Pa. Vol. Inf. Lay all night quiet in camp on the battle-field; a march of 8 miles.

June 27. Left Hoover's Gap, or the rebels retreat from the battle-ground to Fairfield, a march of 5 miles. Made the Johnny's leave their camp and equipage behind and go in haste to save themselves and their army, and followed them up until in sight of Manchester, Coffee county; making them skedaddle again and leave their pickets on post unrelieved. We captured over one hundred prisoners, and encamped for the night, making another march on the same day of 14 miles.

June 28. Marched into Manchester; fell into battle-line and continued so all day. Caught a colonel and sergeant on the bank of the creek, not ten feet from our line of battle. Got marching orders in the evening, left and marched ten miles more the same day, it being Sunday, and making in all a march of 12 miles.

June 29. Left and marched from this camp to Camp Swamp on picket; were rallied at 12 o'clock at night, but it was a false alarm; had a fine night's sleep; a very heavy rain all night. Many troops passing all night to the front; making a march of 6 miles.

June 30. A nice morning, and all quiet in camp: seven miles from Tullahoma due east from here; a man out of Bushe's battery shot himself through the ankle; all quiet in camp.

July 1. Fell in battle-line three times this day, to take up march at 12 o'clock. We started on the Winchester road, Tullahoma having been evacuated by the Johnny rebs, so we encamped for the night. Slept quiet all night at Camp Spring, making a march of 10 miles.

July 2. Left Camp Spring, it being a fine morning, and at 9 o'clock we were on the march toward Bridgeport; skirmished all day more or less. Crossed Elk river; it being very high we had to get two men to volunteer to swim across, taking a cable or rope, used by the batteries, and making one end fast on the other shore we tightened the other end on our side. Both ends of the line being secured, the whole army plunged into the stream to cross, keeping a secure hold of the line, and by overhanding on the rope, to keep those that could not swim from being drowned and keep their heads up out of the water, the whole army of men and horses crossed without losing a man or one accident occurring. The river was so high that we had to leave our whole wagon train back for several days. After crossing formed battle-line and captured five prisoners, and then encamped for the night, making a march of 6 miles.

July 3. Left camp on Elk river Hill; all well and quiet in camp this morning. At 10 o'clock left camp on our march to the battle-field of Wilder's brigade. Turchin in command; found one rebel colonel and a number of our wounded on the battle-field, from a hard fight which took place between the rebel cavalry and the above named Turchin of the Union forces. Having command at that time, and being surrounded by the former, he cut out his way before we reached him and had them on a flying retreat—I mean the rebels; so we encamped for the night on this battle-field, called Camp Turchin, making a march of 1½ miles.

July 4. Left Camp Turchin or battle-field a quarter past 10 o'clock and arrived at Camp Salute on the same day, and took supper and encamped for the night. Gave three cheers and thirty-six salutes from our batteries in behalf of Lee's army being whipped by General Meade's army of the Potomac. Making a march this day of 4 miles.

July 5. Sunday. In the above mentioned camp, and going to lie over for rest. All quiet; the boys enjoying themselves well in foraging a little of almost everything you could mention in the way of eatables.

July 6. Still lying in this same camp. All quiet in camp; one man shot accidentally; nothing else of importance occurred.

July 7. All quiet in camp; a fine morning. At 12 o'clock left this camp and marched west to where there was a graveyard, and encamped. Put up our tents and at 3 o'clock took supper without pies, custards or sweet-cakes, or even Uncle Sam's biscuits, and a pleasant meal it was; so you can guess for yourself what it consisted of. Making a march of 1½ miles.

July 8. Brakefield Point camp is a very nice place; on guard at this place at sun-rise. Heavy salutes given by our batteries for the fall of Vicksburg, and good news of the capture of two thousand prisoners taken and all of Milroy's men re-captured back again; thirty-six rounds fired from every one of our batteries in honor of these glorious news.

July 9. Camp Brakefield Point; came off guard at 9 o'clock, having been relieved; washed my clothes, and ate my dinner, and sat down to note this. Crackers scarce and meat plenty for supper, and have no reason to complain, for fear of worse to come.

July 10. Camp Brakefield Point; a fine dry day; all quiet in camp, and drew full rations of crackers, &c., the first for eight days, the wagon or provision train getting up with us for the first time since crossing Elk river; lying in camp yet four miles from Decker's

Station, Tenn., and sixteen miles from Tullahoma, where Bragg and all his force had to evacuate and just light out.

July 11. In the same camp, and on picket station No. 4, out-post line, second beat from a Presbyterian church, and a Methodist church right across the road from my beat. Making a march of 2 miles.

July 12. Sunday. Came off picket, having been relieved till camp Point Pleasant; looks for rain in the evening. Making a march of 2 miles.

July 13. A fine day. Still in Camp Point Pleasant and all quiet; company inspection in the evening.

July 14. Left Point Pleasant camp and marched past Decker's Station, four miles further, and then on past Cowen's Station one mile, and encamped for the night in Camp Cowen; making in all a march on that day of 12 miles.

July 15. In Camp Cowen; stationed on picket one mile south of the station, No. 1 post, and while there a commissioned officer and a squad of privates passed out on a blackberry excursion; my post of sentinel at a house and used first-rate on this beat; making a march of 2 miles.

July 16. Came off picket, having been relieved from No. 1 post and 2 station, at R. H. Cowen's house, south of the foot of the Cumberland mountains. A fine night of it and a safe return to camp, the 33d Ohio regiment having relieved us; making a march of 2 miles.

July 17. Still in Camp Cowen, and on a detail; all quiet in camp, nothing new occurring worth mentioning.

July 18. In Camp Cowen, and all quiet; not on duty to-day, and the boys digging two wells in camp. General Starkweather having returned to his command after being home on a visit for his health; he looks well, and was received with a hearty welcome by the sons of Uncle Sam's family.

July 19. Detailed in camp this day for supernumerary; took a walk with John Wood about a mile out from camp, a blackberrying. Col. Starkweather returned to his command, and Col. Hambright relieved to the command of his own regiment again. Making a march of 2 miles.

July 20. At the Chattanooga and Tennessee Railroad bridge or stockade, guarding fifteen hundred sacks of corn. Twenty wagons of the 1st brigade and 14th Army corps came for five hundred sacks of it. At breakfast time came off guard, being relieved. A fine morning; making there and back to camp a march of 4 miles.

July 21. Still in Camp Cowen at the foot of the Cumberland mountains; a fine day; detailed out to put up our captain's tent. Our knapsacks and clothing got up with us for the first time for twenty-one days: the first change of clothing for those three weeks or even a clean shirt for that time, and marching through mud and rain all this time.

July 22. Still in Camp Cowen; not on duty to-day, and all quiet in camp. Dug a-while at a well in camp and saw a swarm of bees coming past our camp; stopped them, and put them in a cracker box, and they went to work and did well. Had dress-parade in the evening by Col. H. A. Hambright.

July 23. In the same camp. Company, regimental and brigade inspection. Washed my haversack; detailed for supernumerary in camp guard. A fine day, and now lying between the 24th Ohio regiment, waiting for our turn to move out to the front, as there are many of our troops passing by to-day.

July 24. Still in Camp Cowen. Detailed to go out to the mountains on a foraging expedition, to get a field or two of wheat for provender for our mules and horses. Went out eight miles there and back, making sixteen miles. Got twenty wagon loads of wheat and ten loads of old corn, and a fine feed of blackberries; returned to camp the same day all safe and sound and unmolested, making in all a march of 16 miles.

July 25. Still in Camp Cowen. Detailed to cook beef and make soup for the company to-day. Mike Brannan to be my assistant. Paid in the evening by our captain, J. S. M'Bride, two dollars for back rations, money due each man of an overplus saved by each member of company D.

July 26. Sunday. In the same camp; received my knapsack, but lost my shelter tent. The brass band arrived in our camp from Lancaster city, to join the 79th Regiment of Pa. Vol. Inf., at 3 o'clock in the afternoon, and serenaded our colonel for some time, and was received with a hearty welcome.

July 27. In the same camp; detailed for on outpost picket, No. 1 post and No. 2 station, with our instructions to let no one pass in or out without a proper pass from Generals Sheridan, Brannen, King, Thomas, or Rousseau. A fine day, and making a march out from camp on this day to our posts and stations, without being interrupted in the least, of 5 miles.

July 28. All quiet on our line; relieved by the 33d Ohio regiment off picket on No. 2 station and No. 1 post, and returned again to camp safe and sound, with the news of the famous General John Morgan and all his notorious guerrilla crew captured. Making a march to camp of 5 miles.

July 29. Still in Camp Cowen. All quiet in camp.

July 30. Left Camp Cowen this day at 11 o'clock and moved or changed camp and arrived in Camp Scribner, at the rail road station of the Swanee road; filled two details and helped to pitch our tents; a fine day and making a march of 2 miles.

July 31. In Camp Scribner; on a detail to tear down arbors of Brannen's division to fix some over our officers' tents; very nice day, and nothing new in camp on this day. So ends July month, never to return to us soldiers again.

N. B. This is an inscription on a pointer or fingerboard at Cowen's Station, at the foot of Cumberland mountains, Tenn.: "TO THE UNIVERSITY OF THE SOUTH, AND SHORTEST ROUTE TO THE BEERSHEBA SPRINGS, BY WAY OF SWANEE RAIL ROAD."

On the same day that I copied this inscription I was standing guard over fifteen hundred sacks of corn at a stockade at the above mentioned place. Twenty wagons came for five hundred sacks and had to go back without it, by order of Capt. Wickersham and another quartermaster interfering about it.

Aug. 1. In Camp Scribner; detailed for picket on
5

No. 1 station, at Montgomery Spring, on No. 1 post. A fine day, and all quiet on our line until 9 o'clock at night a man came on horse-back to my post, and after halting him according to the requirements of every sentinel of Uncle Sam's family, I ascertained that he wanted to go to Winchester through our lines. It being against instructions to let any one pass through at that time of the night, I turned him over to the lieutenant of the guard, and he was sent in to head-quarters for examination, and found out to be nothing else than one of John Morgan's spies, and he was dealt with accordingly. Making a march out to this post of 2 miles.

Aug. 2. In Camp Scribner. Returned to camp after being relieved; it being Sunday, all is quiet in camp; we were paid off yesterday two months' pay, twenty-six dollars, in full to the 1st of July, 1863. We had dress-parade in the evening; making a march back to camp again of 2 miles.

Aug. 3. Washed my clothing in the morning; fine day. Had company inspection at 10 o'clock, and dress-parade in the evening. Nothing new occurring in camp of any importance.

Aug. 4. Still in Camp Scribner. Washed my haversack in the morning; lost my pocket-book, went on the search of it and found it with the money taken out by a corporal of Co. K of our regiment; got the money afterward through Fred. Lamin of our company telling me he saw him have the money. So ends this day; a march of 2 miles.

Aug. 5. Still in Camp Scribner. Detailed for picket on No. 2 station and No. 2 post. All quiet on our line all day and night. Had a very nice time of it, and got milk for the first time on picket for our coffee. Making a march out from camp of 2 miles.

Aug. 6. Returned to Camp Scribner, having been relieved from picket by Lieutenant Johnston and a squad of men of the 79th regiment Pa. Vol. Infantry, arriving in camp at 10 o'clock; making a march of 2 miles.

Aug. 7. A fine morning, and still in the same camp. Browned coffee and ground it. Many troops passing by to the front. Eight men out of our regiment detailed out on out-post picket. All quiet in camp.

Aug. 8. A fine morning. Detailed in camp to help clean the streets. Our captain leaving his command in camp, to go to Harrisburg for conscripts on this day.

Aug. 9. Sunday. Detailed in this same camp to go on out-post picket on No. 1 post and No. 2 station, at Montgomery's Ford; and at 2 o'clock had marching orders to leave picket posts at 4 o'clock in the morning and return to camp; making a march of 2 miles.

Aug. 10. Came in off picket, and took up our march at 6 o'clock; making a march of two miles to camp. Ascended the mountains of the Cumberland four miles. Finding ourselves on the wrong road, we right-about and counter-marched back down the mountains two miles, and struck off to the left, and marched all day, the sun being so hot that many of our men fell sun-struck on the road and from the fatigue of their loads. We arrived at a meeting-house and a big spring, and encamped for the night in Camp Dawson; making a march again this day of 15 miles.

Aug. 11. Left Camp Dawson and took up our march of five miles to Anderson's Station, and marched on the same day five more miles to the Alabama line; crossed the line and encamped for the night in Camp Dawson, Alabama; making in all 15 miles.

Aug. 12. Lay all day in camp; very tired and resting seven miles from Stevenson, Ala., on the Chattanooga rail road. Sick all day.

Aug. 13. Washed my clothes, and was excused by our doctor on account of being sick; feel worse in the evening. This valley is called Brunett's Cove, it being between two mountains. Still lying in the same camp.

Aug. 14. Sick in camp, and excused from duty by our doctor. Moved our tents in a different direction. A little better this evening.

Aug. 15. In camp at Brunett's Cove; sick and excused by the doctor from duty for the day. The 24th Ohio regiment of our brigade moved out of our camp across the creek to guard ammunition trains of ours, exposed to the enemy. Nothing new of importance occurred in camp on this day, and all quiet.

Aug. 16. A Sunday in Camp Dawson. Detailed for camp guard on No. 3 post. Raining hard at 12 o'clock; all quiet in camp all day and night. The 1st Wisconsin regiment of our brigade moved to Stevenson Station on this day, seven miles from this camp.

Aug. 17. Came off guard, relieved from duty for the day by a new guard. A fine day, nothing new in camp.

Aug. 18. All quiet in camp. Went out of camp, and got some fine peaches. At 12 o'clock General Negley's troops passed through our camp to the front. A very warm day; making from camp and to it again a march of 3 miles.

Aug. 19. Remaining in the same camp. A fine day; Negley's troops still passing to the front. Roll-call to be eight times a day from this on.

Aug. 20. Detailed for picket at the switch in Brunett's Cove, to guard sanitary stores. Cars passing and re-passing all day with troops of different corps for the front. Forty-three pontoon flats passed in the evening for Bridgeport, to throw a bridge across there. Making a march from camp of 5 miles.

Aug. 21. Relieved from off picket by the 16th regulars, and returned again to camp all safe on this day; making a march back to camp of 5 miles.

Aug. 22. Camp Dawson. Detailed to help sweep off the color line; a fine day and all quiet in camp.

Aug. 23. Detailed from this same camp for out-post picket on No. 2 station and No. 3 post and No. 1 sentinel. All quiet on our line of picket during this day and night; a march of 3 miles.

Aug. 24. Lying in camp; all quiet. Sent to the postmaster at Nashville for some stamped envelopes and received them.

Aug. 25. Relieved from picket by the 18th regulars, and came into camp safe and sound, making a march of 3 miles.

Aug. 26. Had company and regimental inspection in camp.

Aug. 27. Detailed from this camp to out-post picket No. 2 station and No. 3 post and No. 4 sentinel. A fine day, and all quiet on our line of pickets; making a march from camp of 4 miles.

Aug. 28. On the same post and station and sentinel for twelve hours' watch, the night being all quiet. At sun-rise sitting on a log at the reserve post writing a letter, and all quiet at the front of our line of picket.

Aug. 29. Relieved from picket by the 19th Reg. regulars, and returned to camp. Regimental dress-parade until dark; making a march into camp of 4 miles.

Aug. 30. Sunday morning. Off duty; Jacob Ostander of our company received sorrowful news from home—his little child had fallen into the Monongahela river, and its mother, going to the river for its rescue, floated out into deeper water, when her sister on the shore, seeing them about to drown, jumped in to save them, and all three were lost. So on this day he leaves camp on a furlough to his once happy home, but now one of sorrow to him.

Aug. 31. Detailed from Camp Dawson to go on out-post picket on No. 2 station, No. 3 post and No 2 sentinel. The regulars all on the move to the front at 2 o'clock of this day. So another month ends. Making a march from camp of 1½ miles.

Sept. 1. Relieved from picket by the 24th Ohio regiment; came into camp all safe; a fine day; making a march into camp of 1½ miles.

Sept. 2. Left Camp Dawson, Jackson county, Ala., and took up our march. Came to Stevenson, seven miles of a march, and moved on to Bridgeport. Sick all day and all night. Encamped for the night in sight of the Tennessee river, near Bridgeport; in all making a march on this day of 18 miles.

Sept. 3. Bridgeport camp. Lying in camp, all quiet. The trestle-bridge has been broken down on the south of the island in the Tennessee river at this port, so that we cannot cross until it is repaired by our army, which will soon be accomplished, as our men are busily at work, and Uncle Sam don't care for expenses.

Sept. 4. Camp near Bridgeport. Struck tents at twenty minutes past 2 o'clock, and crossed the Tennessee river to the island. At 4 o'clock in the evening began crossing on the pontoons, the pontoon-bridge being 175 yards long, and the trestle-bridge on the south side of the island 360 yards long. We made the crossing safe with our whole army, and encamped for the night on the shore of the Tennessee river, in a secesh camp, they having had to get up and dust; making a march this day of 3 miles.

Sept. 5. Left the river and took up our march into Hog Jaw Valley, at the entering of Shellmound Mountain Gap, and encamped at Moore's big spring, well known by the surrounding country there, or any one ever passing it will remember it by this name, for the great flow of water coming right out from under this mountain, which is thousands of feet high. The name of the valley originated, I was told, by one of its early settlers, by a man passing through it on what is termed the old Indian trail road from Sand Mountain, in early days, to see some land in Sequatchey Valley, and on his journey through this valley he stopped at a house or family by the name of Smith, and asking for something to eat, was not refused by this generous family. But as most of you know, at that time folks were not provided with all the dainties and luxuries of life like in these days; so on this occasion a hog's jaw and some peas were served up for the guest's dinner, and after leaving, not receiving anything for this, the settler termed or christened it Hog Jaw Valley. This is the source from whence originated its name.

Sept. 6. Sunday in camp at Moore's big spring, in Hog Jaw Valley, at the foot of Shellmound mountain, Georgia. Detailed out with our company to guard and take care of one hundred and two cattle at 10 o'clock; received them in our charge or care one-half a mile from our camp, and found them in a lot of ground of about five acres, in which we kept them until about 5 o'clock in the evening, when orders came for us to let them out and drive them some two miles further down the valley and let them graze till 12 o'clock at night of the same day, to give the whole army and trains time to get up this above named mountain, before we would start. At 12 o'clock at night we came back up the valley two miles, to the foot of the mountain, and followed up the mountains after our train, until about half way up, when, owing to the steepness and warm day and dust—equal to any snow for depth that I ever saw—a great many of our mules and horses had given out, and were unloosened and turned in for the night, barricading the road perfectly up with them and the wagons. So we managed to get past them with the cattle, and went on all night and arrived on the morning of the 7th at Saw Mill bridge on Silver creek, and were relieved by an Ohio company from our charge or guard; making a march in all of 13½ miles.

Sept. 7. Silver creek, Saw Mill bridge. Relieved by the 24th Ohio from guarding cattle. This same morning took up our march again over the mountains nine miles to Lookout Valley, and encamped three miles from Trenton, Georgia, where General Negley and his forces had arrived before us and captured two hundred prisoners; making a march in all on this day of 9 miles.

Sept. 8. Lookout Valley camp. The first three companies of the 79th regiment detailed to work on or repair this valley road, so we could move down the valley with our whole army; so we fixed up our tents, and all is quiet in camp in the evening, making a march out of camp and back again of 2 miles.

Sept. 9. Still in the same camp. Detailed out on camp duty or guard all night; all quiet on my post No. 1.

Sept. 10. Camp Lookout Valley. Good news in camp this morning: Chattanooga and Rome in our possession. Relieved of camp guard by another company; this being in Date county, three miles from Trenton, Ga.

Sept. 11. Camp Lookout Valley. Took up our march again from this place at 6 o'clock in the morning, and marched to within sight of Fox Mountain to Niggertown, and awaited further orders; got dinner and took up our march again, and marched ten miles further on to the entering of a valley called Johnston's Bend, and encamped for the night; making a march in all this day of 16 miles.

Sept. 12. Camp at the entering of Johnston's Bend. Took up our march again or left from this camp at 5 o'clock in the morning, and was detained till 12 o'clock with our wagon train going up Lookout mountain. Marched over this mountain to where General Negley had to fall back with his forces, being overpowered. So we encamped for the night, making a march on this day in all of 7 miles.

Sept. 13. Johnston's Bend camp, Negley's retreat. Lying in camp all day, marching orders came but were countermanded again at 1 o'clock. Detailed in the evening to go to the mountains to draw grub for our regiment; making to and from camp this day a march of 4 miles.

Sept. 14. Johnston's Bend camp, Walker county, Ga. Detailed for out-post picket on No. 1 station, No. 1 post, under charge of Lieut. Mccasky. All quiet on our line of picket, near Dug Gap; making from our camp to our line of picket a march on this day of 2 miles.

Sept. 15. Johnston's Bend, near Dug Gap. Relieved from off No. 1 post and No. 1 station, by the 24th Ohio regiment. Returned again to camp at 9 o'clock all safe and sound, and drew rations for one day; making a march back to camp on this day of 2 miles.

Sept. 16. Camp near Johnston's Bend. Moved or

changed front of our camp; lay all day quiet in camp. Orders came at dark to take up our march on the following morning at 7 o'clock, and leave this camp. So ends this day.

Sept. 17. Left camp at Johnston's Bend and took up our march again at 7 o'clock this morning; marched to the front six miles to Chattanooga Valley. Right smart cannonading in the south direction of the enemy. Making a march of 6 miles.

Sept. 18. Chickamauga creek camp. Fell in battle-line at 4 o'clock in the morning; heavy cannonading on our left at 12 o'clock; at 4 o'clock in the evening got marching orders and left this camp in a hurry for the front, and marched six miles to Rosencrans' headquarters, or to Camp Big Spring, near the above mentioned spring, or Dug Gap, where our forces the day before had a hard fight with the enemy and succeeded in driving them back or holding them in check till our arrival. So we encamped for the night; making a march of 6 miles.

Sept. 19. Slept three hours after encamping in the above mentioned camp, and then took up our march to the battle-ground of Chickamauga, which was fought on the 19th and 20th of this month. This was the hardest battle fought by us since the war began. We arrived on the ground this morning at 4 o'clock, in time to prevent the enemy from getting in to this road ahead of us; so they drew their artillery and all their forces back off the road at this point into a thick woods, and waited till daylight. After falling into battle-line and posting out-post pickets and videttes, we were ordered to cook our breakfasts; so at it we went, for we were both hungry and tired, after marching all night, making a march of eight miles. No sooner were we ready to partake of those luxuries of life, without which we could not subsist, than the ball was opened on our left, and soon our whole force was personally engaged. At 10 o'clock we were ordered forward on a charge with our brigade and whole division, and soon became engaged. Having been outflanked by the enemy, we lost six pieces of artillery for a short time, and a great many men, but soon re-captured our artillery. Fought hard all day till after dark. At 9 o'clock we were ordered forward to cover Col. Johnston's regiment with a skirmish line, as Longstreet's corps had reinforced the rebels and had attacked Col. Johnston's regiment. By some misunderstanding, and the night being dark, at our approach to his line, thinking the enemy had outflanked them, he ordered three companies to be turned on us, mowing us down like sheep, and many of us making narrow escapes. Lieut. Col. Miles of our regiment had his horse shot from under him and was taken prisoner at this time, having been rendered unfit to fight on foot or to get out of their way, on account of having had his leg broken some time previous to this fight, which you have read of in the first pages of this book. So he (Col. Miles) had to share the fate of the one penning these lines, being marched afterward, with many others, to the well-known Libby Prison, Richmond, Virginia, and crowded in those filthy and polluted pens, worse than our pig-sties at home; officers having little more privilege than privates. So we were called off the battle-ground at 10 o'clock of this same night, and all became quiet for the night, with the exception of the groans of the wounded and bleeding and dying on the battle-ground, to whom we could render no assistance, on account of the rebels holding the battle-ground and us. Our line unbroken on this day, and encamped for the night; making in all a march of 7 miles.

Sept. 20. Camp near battle-ground. At 4 o'clock in the morning, after having a good night's sleep and unmolested rest, we were ordered to fall into battle-line, march to a certain point, and take our position before daylight, this being Sunday morning. Having accomplished this, we cooked our breakfasts, and after partaking thereof, Col. Starkweather, a resident of Wisconsin, and our brigade commander, got orders to send out a skirmish-line one hundred yards to feel the enemy and their position, to see if we could remove the dead and wounded off the ground. After our skirmish-line had proceeded one hundred yards unmolested, we were ordered one hundred yards further to the front, and arriving there unmolested, we were ordered one hundred yards still further on by the same General; but before reaching this last line we became engaged with a skirmish-line of the rebels, consisting of part of Longstreet's, Ewell's, Humphrey's and Cheatham's corps, and soon the ball was open again for this day. The whole army became personally engaged. On the enemy came in a solid mass of corps after corps, driving in our skirmish-line after line, but their places were soon filled by our brave boys. Our brigade being in the centre of our line, we were ordered to hold it at all hazards. On the enemy came, charge after charge, with the cheer of Bull Run, but we let them know there was no Bull Run there, slaughtering them by our well aimed shots of shell, canister, grape and musketry by hundreds; I would be safe in saying by thousands they fell while trying to break our lines in those charges, and failing to accomplish their designs, they would change their front line, first right-oblique and then left-oblique, turning their faces sideways against the storm of our bullets—such as you who read these lines have often witnessed in case of snow storms or blustery weather at home, in quiet times and peaceful hours. But not so on this occasion. Charge after charge was made upon us, but they failed to break our line, or to even get us confused in the least. So they swung their line around right and left of us, leaving us until the afternoon, with the exception of sharp-shooters, who annoyed us now and again, killing and wounding but few of us, with the exception of our skirmish-line. General Starkweather was wounded through the fleshy part of the calf of the leg early in the day, by a sharp-shooter of the rebels hitting him with a minnie ball, rendering him very lame; yet the brave commander would not flinch from his duty, but stuck to us and his command throughout the fight. Many of their lines came in and gave themselves up during this time, assuring our General that it was just a stampede in the morning, and that they would give us hark in the evening. They were fighting hard on our right and left all this day. In the afternoon our right and left line had to fall back some three-quarters of a mile to establish a new line, and in doing this we were exposed to the enemy. Soon we were engaged again, this being at 3 o'clock in the afternoon; and such fighting I never saw before nor since. In the meanwhile we were surrounded and our ammunition cut off from us; and as soon as what remained became exhausted, and our line established in our rear, we got orders to prepare to retreat. No sooner had we received these orders than General Baird, commanding our division, came along and gave orders for us to retreat; so in a few moments we were all falling back, being surrounded and cut off from our ammunition. We were ordered to halt at a crib of rails and logs thrown up in rear of the first line some twenty yards, and used in the fore part of this day to protect our reinforcements in coming up. We were ordered at the time of halt to rally to save our men in the rear from being pushed so hard on their retreat; but owing to the confused state and excitement of some of the men, as well as the fact that the lieutenant who was acting captain of our company, in place of our captain absent at home on detailed duty, took leg-bail and cut for safer quarters, leaving us and many others to the mercy of the result of this retreat. So through the misfortune of not doing as some did, run, we were surrounded, not knowing the line had fallen back, and were captured at this place and time. At sundown of this day, four of our company and twenty-nine of our regiment were captured; I was taken by the rebel Col. Humphrey's men and turned over by them to a guard of Longstreet's corps to take us in charge, and was sent to the rear seven miles to Cheatham's headquarters or hospital, called Rock Spring, and encamped for the night, for the first time, with rebel sentinels around our camp.

This is my capture as near as I can make it known to you, and a sorrowful one to me it was, as you will see further on in these pages—which would cause the world to stand in amazement, and the animal family to fall, under the starvation and cruel treatment of those filthy, polluted and crowded pens or places of confinement, which the human family are exposed to while in the jaws and hands of the so-called Southern Confederacy; and especially the poor private Union soldier whose misfortune it is to fall into their hands in this way—which I am not able to describe to you by pen and ink, nor can any artist paint, or tongue give utterance in full, without being challenged. But having come through the sensation and feelings of these awful items set forth before you, I have to believe it is so, and give or present to you this as a true copy for your consideration; which I am willing to give an account of to the great I Am, when pen and ink will be no more, and I shall cease from all labors and trials of this world, and rest in peace for ever and ever.

Sept. 21. Camp Cheatham's Hospital, or rather his headquarters, well known by the writer as Rock Spring camp, in the Southern Confederacy so-called, in Georgia, about seven miles from Chickamauga battle-ground surrounded by a heavy guard of rebels. So on this morning each and every man's name, company, regiment, rank, residence, and birth-place was taken by a rebel lieutenant and registered in one of their books of record; and afterward you could see rebel citizens with double-barreled shot-guns, rifles, pistols, sabres, old scythes, made something similar to our corn-cutters at home, and almost every thing you could mention, and in a short time we were turned over from the first guard to this second one just spoken of. Soon a double square was formed by these hardened wretches, and six hundred and two of us privates marched into this same square, and also one hundred of our officers shared the same fate and were marched into this same square, and marched from this camp ten miles to Ringgold, and there our names were again taken with company, regiment, and so on, and we were turned over to another guard. Many of their troops were passing through this town at the same time to reinforce their army at the front. So after having all fixed up according to military tactics, we were marched further on foot seven miles to Tunnel Hill Station, and drew our first rations in the so-called Southern Confederacy, being allowed one tin-cup of cornmeal and two ounces of old meat to each man for three days' rations, and had to bake it ourselves the best way we could, or eat it in the meal, without salt or anything else.

Sept. 22. Left Camp Tunnel Hill, Walker county, Ga., and was marched on foot to Dalton, where we encamped for the night, and in a short time after were ordered to fall into line and prepare to march. We were marched through town, up one street and down another for some time, with the shouts from every house, "Look at the damned Yankees!" After some time we were marched back to the same camp for want of conveyance to send us further on; making a march in all on this day, from the one place to the other and in this last town, of 9 miles.

Sept. 23. Wheatfield county, Dalton Station camp. Left this camp and was marched to town and shipped on cars the same as our cattle are crowded in at the drove-yards at home; and I would be safe in saying, in as much filth and with as hard treatment. Hundreds of poor Union soldiers were crowded into these cars at this place and time, who were so unfortunate as to fall into their hands by being surrounded and captured in this way. After being shipped aboard the cars, we were sent on nine miles to Resaca, and seven miles further on to Calhoun Station, also five miles further to Andersonville Station, and also ten miles more to Gordonville Station, Calhoun county-seat Kingston, and also further ten miles on to the junction of the Rome rail road, Barren county, also farther on to Cass Station; a march of 4 miles.

Sept. 24. Atlanta, Ga., camp. A fine morning. Drew three crackers for rations for one day; searched, and every thing of apparel or wear taken from us, even to the spoon, knife and fork we ate with, and put into a yard or bull-pen made with planks twenty feet long set upright on end, taking in acres of ground in this way; a heavy guard was set all around the outside of said pen and sentinels placed on an upright scaffold, so as to look down into the inside, and see what we were doing. So we were kept in this place all the night of this same day; making a march of 8 miles.

Sept. 25. Left Atlanta at 8 o'clock of this day and came to Augusta, a march of two hundred and three miles, and encamped for the night in a church yard or park. We saw in this town the negroes of the South shut up in buildings by hundreds, to be sold to the highest bidder, just as we sell our cattle or chattels in our States at public sale. Staid all night in this camp till 8 o'clock. Drew three crackers of hard-tack for one day's rations.

Sept. 26. In Church Yard Park camp, Augusta, having remained in this camp all night, and were shipped aboard of cattle cars again in all the filth and dirt, the cattle having been removed and us placed in their vacant room, at 8 o'clock on this morning, and left under a heavy guard on the Charleston rail road. Ran all day and night very slow, being a very heavy train, and came up this road to within sixty-nine miles of Charleston, and then took the South Carolina rail road at Branchville; making a march of eighty-four miles. South Carolina.—Still continuing on our journey, on the same cars. A fine warm day. Saw rice growing, and a great many other curiosities; almost suffocated to death, being crowded so thickly in the box cars with all the filth that mortal eye could behold, and nothing to eat this day but one ear of corn for three of us, to be shelled and divided amongst us, and then grind it with our own teeth, and eat it which ever way you pleased, to keep you from starving; making in all a march of 137 miles.

Sept. 27. Sunday morning. Took breakfast at a rosin factory, six miles from Columbia, Richland Co.

Came on still further to Charlottetown in North Carolina; making a march of 110 miles.

Sept. 28. Charlottetown, North Carolina, ten miles in this State; at 3 o'clock in the afternoon were **crowded into another train of cars, and got to** Haw river, **one hundred** and nineteen miles, **or a** place called Company Shops; making in all a march on this day of 129 miles.

Sept. 29. **Company Shops at or** near Haw river. Moved slowly forward **on this** day, the rail road being **in bad order and a heavy train;** we arrived in the afternoon at Raleigh, **the capital of North** Carolina. Drew rations for two days—moulded hard-tack and old **bacon—never before saw the like of it, nor any of my** brother soldiers with me, since **the day we were born;** no one could tell the material or ingredients they were made of; **we could not eat them; they were so hard** we couldn't chew them, **and we couldn't** soften them with water. Although **starvation was staring us in the** face, and hunger, the **mother of a craving** appetite, **we were compelled to resign ourselves to** eight of those **mentioned crackers and** a small piece of stinking meat, say from two to three ounces, for those two days' rations above mentioned; and you might eat it or starve, which ever you pleased. We were shipped at 11 o'clock at **night on** another train of cars **on** the Louisburg rail road; making in all a march **at this time** of 65 miles.

Sept. 30. Left Raleigh at 11 o'clock at night, and came sixty-five miles to Baker's Station, and thirty-nine miles further to **the junction of the** Weldon rail road, and also sixty-three and one-half miles further to Petersburg, and were marched through this town on foot, sixteen hundred of us, and put on another train of cars about an hour before sundown, and came twelve miles further during the night. Got into Richmond, Va., at 12 o'clock at night, and after being marched down through town until in front of the so-called and well known Libby Prison, we were halted, and being well guarded, were ordered to surrender up to them all of our wearing apparel, but what we had on our backs, that had not been taken from us previous to this, and all money or any thing about our person, even to the spoons, knives and forks we formerly used to eat with. Some refusing to do so, were introduced to a building of old Libby's, called Smith's building, and marched into the first cell or floor of this building, one by one passing in the same way, being thoroughly searched by those inhuman wretches, until perfectly filled—passing from one floor to the other till there were three hundred men on each floor. There being three floors, there were nine hundred of us crowded into this one building, three hundred feet long and twenty-four feet wide, without fire, or any kind of furniture to either sit or lie down on, but a rough plank floor, even in the coldest time of frost and winter—without any clothing but what we had upon us to protect us through these cold nights; and all the comfort we had was to lay our weary heads upon a brick stolen or pried out of the wall of said prison for a pillow. As these buildings had been used since the war began for confining the deserters of their own army in, and afterward for us poor Union soldiers, after being captured through the misfortune of war, these crowded and filthy pens were inhabited by a living family, that tormented you day and night, from which you could not escape or get rid of, and with no change of clothes; I might say they were not single but married, with large families, moving up and down on the joists, rafters and floors so thick that you could not help interrupting them on their journey for a new sit; and any one who hoped to prevent them from increasing on him must spend at least one hour a day butchering them, or die in this kind of filth.

Oct. 1. In Smith's building prison, on Cary street, Richmond, Va., guarded by a heavy guard of infantry around the outside as well as in the inside, and batteries placed on every street and knoll commanding and covering said building. Drew rations for one day, being allowed ten ounces of wheat bread to each man for twenty-four hours, with a small allowance of water, without coffee or anything in lieu of it, or anything else. So ends this day, and we to be content with our lot.

Oct. 2. Still in the same prison. Rained all night. Nothing new occurring worthy of note. It being 2 o'clock, the time has arrived for drawing rations, and I can assure you that hunger is good sauce for a hungry appetite, and it being a small piece of meat and bread, as above spoken of, daily issued to me and my fellow prisoner soldiers, you who read these lines stop and consider, when I tell you on this day, and from this on. we could see starvation staring us in the eyes for the want of food, and the frosts of coming winter making themselves already visible to us in these crowded, filthy and polluted cells. And I am safe in saying to you, that we were searched and stripped of all our clothing, blankets and wearing apparel except that on our bodies, all other being taken from us by those inhuman wretches and us left to freeze or die in this state, as hundreds did, as you will see further on in these pages, by starvation and want of clothing, which I am not able to describe unto you in full without being challenged; nor can any artist paint or tongue give utterance to the extreme reality of the cruel, hard treatment we are and have to undergo. And now having come through these awful feelings and sensations caused by this kind of treatment, I have to believe it is so—and leave these few lines with you for your consideration, and to decide for yourselves if my representation be true or not.

Oct. 3. All well in our floor. Still in the same prison. Having gone to bed without supper, and got up without breakfast, and done without dinner, it has come to the usual hour for drawing the rations allowed us once every twenty-four hours, and little at that, as I have already told you. I will now tell you the reason for our missing eating these meals above spoken of, and a good reason I think it is for doing so long without—and God only knows how we did do without so long, for I can't tell you—but I can tell you how some tried to do, to save those small rations when drawn to make three meals of: they and I would divide our small portions into three equal parts before eating any of it, considering it was to make us three meals in twenty-four hours, and would lay it down on the floor beside us, as we had no other place of safety to keep it, taking up one portion for supper, as we drew but once each day at 3 o'clock in the afternoon, thinking to save the other two parts for breakfast and dinner on the coming day; but our hunger being so great, we could not help taking up the second part intended for breakfast, and the more we would look at it the hungrier we would feel; after pinching or picking small pieces off around the edge, piece after piece, till almost exhausted, down it would go—the same as all of us have witnessed of the babe or child given sweetmeats, which at first would try to save it, but through the temptation of taste and appetite could not help eating it up. But not so with us precisely, for here was the third part yet in reserve for the coming dinner, but for dinner it never could be withheld, for before bed-time this third part would be eaten in like manner. Then you can see us, finding we could not resist the temptations of hunger and starvation enough to make three meals, we would make one out of it, and not satisfied then, we would have to resign ourselves to our hard fate, and be content with our lot and misfortune of being captured and confined in these filthy cells, inhabited by a living family, such as I never saw before nor since, which would cause us to spend two hours daily to butcher or slaughter them, as we could not stand their attacks upon us—which would cause the animal family to sink under them, if not rid of them, as we had to do to keep them from becoming so numerous upon us.

Oct. 4. Sunday morning. Still in the same prison and closely guarded by a heavy force. At daylight a man belonging to the 5th Indiana battery, name unknown to me, died on our floor from starvation and cold, for nothing else under the heavens caused his death but this; he died without a struggle and very suddenly, being composed and resigned to his hard lot. without a relative or friend near him but his captured brother soldiers; and little could we do for him, sharing the same fate of cruel treatment, confined with him. This is the first instance of death among us since our confinement in this awful situation, and a sorrowful one for any one to witness, shut up in a polluted and filthy prison, from friends and home. But we hope our loss may be his infinite gain.

Oct. 5. Monday morning. Still in the same prison. A very cool day and raining, and we are shivering with cold, and not allowed the least fire. Oh, if I could only tell you the awful hunger and cold that we have to endure in this place to-day, after having been brought down from rich and plenty to a mere nothing. and to be contented with a rough floor to sit or lie down on, or stand up, or any way you could see fit, for neither clothes nor furniture of any kind were allowed us to make us in the least comfortable. God knows we were used worse than our swine or dumb brutes are at home.

Oct. 6. Still in the same prison. Drew hard-tack for one day's rations, being four small crackers to each man, and a small piece of meat, say two inches square, and hellish at that. I cannot compare it to anything I can think of only our scraps and pieces of waste meat saved for the manufacture of soap, and about the same for smell and taste.

Oct. 7. Still in the same prison. Drew one day's rations of soft bread, being allowed a common five cent loaf of baker's bread to four men for twenty-four hours, with a small portion of salt meat, and the water the meat was cooked in for our drink in place of coffee or tea. The lower floor got into a fight or muss about some bread; one man got badly hurt.

Oct. 8. Still in the same prison. Drew on this day a quarter of a five cent baker's loaf to each man, and a small portion of meat, and hard stuff at that; all disgusted at our grub, so that we can hardly eat any of it—our appetites becoming poor from want of vegetables and the necessary comforts of life in this unhappy place of confinement. But so it is—we have to be content with our lot; let it be ever so hard, we must be resigned to our fate.

Oct. 9. Still in the same prison. Rations the same, scant and poor at that. Necessity is said to be the mother of invention, and in this case of starvation we were compelled to ferret out some substitute for provisions to keep us alive, or we should die for want of food: so at it we went. There was a basement story or cellar underneath our cells, and so closely shut up or darkened that nothing could be seen in it by the inmates of the prison, and no entrance from our apartments into it; after a consultation amongst us we contrived to tear off of the floor some sheet iron, which had been used previous to our admittance to this place under the stove, to prevent the burning of the floor, and we managed to fit out a knife and by this means cut a plank out of the floor, so as to let a man down to ascertain what was concealed therein. We found it to contain sugar by the hogshead full, and a great deal of salt; so we concluded to deal out our own rations in this case. We drew the sugar out of the hogsheads at night, and issued one quart of sugar to each man daily, as a substitute for the coffee and tea we were deprived of previous to this. We succeeded for some time in this way, and got along well for two weeks, relieving the rebels of a few pounds less than twenty tons before discovered. When any of the officers would enter our building on business, we would manage for some one to be lying on the hole cut through the floor, as though he was sick, thus hiding the place from detection. After some time the sewers of our sinks became foul and turned into the cellar above spoken of, and going in to see if any damage was done therein, they found nineteen hogsheads already emptied. We expected to be placed in the dungeon of Castle Thunder or some other place of punishment. The remainder of the sugar was soon moved out of the cellar, and all they said about it, was: "It was a sly joke of the Yankees."

Oct. 10. A fine day. Still in the same prison. All tolerably well on our floor to-day. Drew rations of about the same, hard enough I can assure you; but recovered some from our weak state by the use of the sugar and salt discovered in the cellar and used by us.

Oct. 11. Still in the same prison. A fine warm morning; roll-call every morning at 8 o'clock about as usual. Some very sick on the middle and lower floors. Saw a number of our men carried from another prison, who had died to-day; they were removed by negroes in a careless manner. I saw one carried by three of these beings and let fall on the street, breaking the coffin or box, letting the dead body fall out upon the street; no sooner was the dead man out than one of those black rascals caught the dead body by the feet, taking the bottom of the coffin to haul him, using him more like a brute than a human being. Two of them afterward took the body upon their shoulders, the other gathered up the rest of the pieces and started down Cary street. This was the last I saw of my poor brother soldier's remains treated in this manner; and many others treated as bad, have I been witness of. God forgive those inhuman wretches.

Oct. 12. In the same prison. Drew hard bread and I might say hard meat too, and but little of that, for this day's rations. A fine day. The city bells gave alarm of fire in the morning, a house and machine shop being destroyed by it.

Oct. 13. In the same prison. Wrote a letter to my daughter Sarah Emiline Johnston, informing her of my capture on the 20th of September. Drew rations of the same; hard enough, I can assure you.

Oct. 14. Drew hard bread and meat, as usual, on this day. Rained a little; all forenoon cloudy; at 12 o'clock looks for rain. Drew soup for the first time, and you couldn't guess what it was made of, I couldn't, for there was never seen the like since John was a baby.

Oct. 15. In the same prison. Drew soft bread and bacon meat for this day's rations. Rained all forenoon, afternoon clear and pleasant. You who read these lines may think, because the amount of rations is not enumerated or the kind is not specified each and every day, that some days we might fare pretty well; but, gentlemen and ladies, I can't say so; for paper, or time, or place, will not permit me to describe in full, nor will I attempt to give you in full the reality. But one thing I can say to you, I have seen the time, yes, and thousands others, that we thought, if we had had the privilege of remaining in our pig-sties at home and feed from the swill-tub, we would feel as though we were admitted into a king's palace.

Oct. 16. In the same prison. Drew soft bread and salt meat for this day's rations. Rained all day.

Oct. 17. In the same prison. Feel pretty well. Drew soft bread, the quarter of a five cent baker's loaf to each man for twenty-four hours' rations, and one ounce of salt meat for the same time. You who read these pages and are at home in rich and plenty, eating at your own table covered with all the luxuries of life, until your appetites are satisfied, just think for one moment of our awful situation; when our small allowance was eaten up, we could get no more, and well we knew it; and Oh the gnawing sensation at our stomachs for the want of food to keep us from starvation, and to know that we could get no more.

Oct. 18. In the same prison. Drew soft bread and meat, as described to you before, for this day's rations. On this day we found a pile of bran concealed in the cellar of our prison, and I can tell you it was a happy find to us. Water passing through our cells, we could get free use of it to mix the bran up, as we have often done at home to feed the cows and swine; and we ate it in like manner, without salt or fire added thereto; and I tell you it was a fine dish to us, to satisfy our hungry and gnawing appetites. You may think this a big saying, but I have felt and tasted it, and have to believe it is so.

Oct. 19. Libby Prison, Smith's building, on Cary street, Richmond, Va. Drew soft bread and salt meat as usual for this day's rations, and still using our bran slop in addition to our small rations, to keep our weak frames from falling under the cruel treatment endured in these filthy and polluted cells.

Oct. 20. In the same prison. A nice day. Drew soft wheat bread and a small ration of beef, and still using our stolen wheat bran as slop, with our small rations, and have to be very thankful that it was so ordered that we got it in time to save us.

Oct. 21. In the same prison, and no prospect of being released, this being our twenty-first day here. A fine cool day, and not allowed fire at all. Drew our small ration of soft bread and meat for this day.

Oct. 22. Same prison. A cloudy day. Drew soft bread and salt meat, and the water the meat was boiled in, for one day's rations.

Oct. 23. Same prison. Drew four hard-tack crackers, and say two inches square of old meat, and hard stuff at that; a cool day all through. Two hundred prisoners fetched in under guard by the Johnnies from Rosencrans' army at 12 o'clock to-day.

Oct. 24. Libby Prison. Drew soft bread and meat for this day's rations. Rained all day and very cool. Suffering very much from cold, and no fire allowed us.

Oct. 25. In the same prison. Drew for this day's rations soft bread and our usual allowance of meat. A very cool day.

Oct. 26. In the same prison. A very cool and dry day. Drew soft bread and salt meat for this day. To-day it was found out that we were using the Johnnies' concealed bran, and they removed it out of our reach. So this leaves us still worse off for food than ever.

Oct. 27. Same prison. Drew soft bread and meat for this day's rations; good on this day, but very small in quantity. A fine clear day.

Oct. 28. In the same prison. In good health, but very weak from want of food, and nothing else. Drew very good wheat bread and a small portion of beef for this day's rations.

Oct. 29. Same prison. Drew soft bread and the same of meat for this day. A clear and cool day; many of our men suffering from cold and want of clothing.

Oct. 30. Same prison. Drew on this day soft bread and salt meat for our rations. A cool clear day all through.

Oct. 31. Same prison. Drew soft bread and old meat for this day's rations. A wet forenoon, clear at dinner time, but looks for rain this evening. So ends this month.

Nov. 1. In the same prison. Drew on this day

soft bread and one ounce of beef to each man for his rations. A fine clear day all through.

Nov. 2. Same prison, and have been all this time without fire or clothes sufficient to keep us warm, with nothing to lie down on but a rough plank floor, and wet, dirty and filthy at that; and nothing to sit on except you would loosen a brick out of the wall, and then you could use it for both seat and pillow, until an officer would come in and take it from you.

Nov. 3. In the same prison. Drew on this day for rations soft bread and a small portion of meat, and hellish at that—the scent of it made the most of us halloo New York at the approach of it into our cells, although our hunger was great. It was inhabited by a living family trying to remove the meat from the bone. God only knows how we did live this long, for I could not tell if you were to ask me.

Nov. 4. A fine clear day, and still in the same prison. Drew soft bread and one ounce of salt meat for this day's rations.

Nov. 5. A clear and cool day. Drew bread, a mixture of potatoes with it, but at no time any salt in it, with a small portion of good beef.

Nov. 6. A dull cool day, and still in the same prison. Drew soft bread and sweet potatoes mixed and baked together, and a small piece of salt meat, for this day's rations.

Nov. 7. In the same prison. Drew bread of the same mixture and a small bit of meat, and hard stuff at that. I have often at home and abroad, when I had plenty to eat, wondered, when I would see my own or my neighbor's dog gnawing at a bone of any kind, what good or substance they could get out of it, but not so now with me; for in these days, confined in these prisons, I and all of us have gnawed in like manner at them, eating the bone so far as soft enough to be chewed, and then smashing it with something and sucking it till our mouths would become so sore with the roughness that we could not try to feed our hungry appetites and keep us from starving. I don't wonder in the least at the animal, when human beings have had to do the same, and thousands of our prisoners this day would laugh with joy if they could get a bone to do likewise, as we have had to do to save our once almost hopeless lives.

Nov. 8. A cool and cloudy day. In the same prison. Drew soft bread and beef for this day's rations.

Nov. 9. In the same prison. A cool raw day. Drew the same kind of bread and a small piece of meat, and not good at that.

Nov. 10. A clear and cold day. In the same prison. Drew soft bread, and one ounce of beef a piece to each man for this day's rations.

Nov. 11. In the same prison. On this day drew corn bread, one pound to each man, and a spoonful of rice, without salt or anything else to it.

Nov. 12. In the same prison. Drew for our rations corn and potatoes mixed and baked together, without salt, and a spoonful of so-called negro beans, something similar to our peas, only black.

Nov. 13. Still in the so-called Libby Prison. Drew

rice cooked without salt, or anything else added thereto, but water, and corn bread baked in like manner, and hard stuff at that, I can assure you who read these few lines. This morning were ordered to fall into line the same as at usual roll-call heretofore, by order of the rebel general having charge of us on this post, his name unknown to me, and counting off from the right of the line one hundred and sixty men, telling us that they would be sent away from this prison to-day and the same number to-morrow, not knowing where to, but we found out afterwards; and thinking we would be searched before leaving, you should have seen the bran in little piles through that building left for fear of being found on or about our persons. You will remember, as you have seen already in these pages, that we had stolen it from the basement story of our prison, and used it like slop or swill to save our fast wasting frames from starvation—from starving to death I might say, for we could already see it staring us in the face, and in our midst daily. From each and every one of these prisons we could see our brother soldiers removed out to the dead-house, not knowing how soon it would be our lot to follow to that same bourne from whence no traveler returns, where the weary are at rest and cease from all their troubles. And Oh, to think, by starvation and ill-treatment from those inhuman wretches, and nothing else under the heavens, and far away from home or friends, to die in this condition, without one word of consolation, but to be resigned to our fate! On this same day they moved us across the street into another building of a similar kind to that we had been kept in, to get us away from the bran, saying, "You Yanks will and can do anything, and we will put a stop to it here." A clear nice day.

Nov. 14. Still in Richmond prison. A cool morning, and without fire or even comfortable clothing, and almost starved, going to bed without supper and getting up without breakfast, for the reasons I have already given you. This morning drew one loaf of corn and potatoes mixed and baked in bread for the trip, being sent from this place to Danville, one hundred and forty miles south-west from Richmond. Ran slowly all day and night and got to our place of destination at 8 o'clock in the morning of the 15th.

Nov. 15. Arrived here safe this morning, after running a march of one hundred and forty miles, shut up in cattle cars and treated worse than cattle by the guard over us. Raining all night, and very cool; we were almost frozen, and now again shut up in an open frame building, three stories high, one hundred and forty feet long and twenty-four feet wide, without fire or anything else to make us feel in the least comfortable, and inhabited by a living family to torment us day and night, of which we could not get rid of in these filthy pens or cells, which would cause the animal family to fall and the world to stand in amazement, to know that some of us lived through it all; and Oh, I might say, how very few indeed there are to tell you these sad news from this place.

Nov. 16. In the same prison, being the second day in Danville Prison, No. 2, Va., situated on the bank of the Dan river. Drew three ounces of salt meat and a five cent loaf of cane-seed bread for this day's rations, so bitter in taste that we could hardly eat it, but starving to death is good sauce for an appetite to a man, when the animal family would refuse to eat our diet here.

Nov. 17. In the same prison. Drew for this day's rations half a loaf of bread of the same kind above spoken of, and hard stuff, I can assure you. A very cool day, and many of us sick.

Nov. 18. In the same prison. The same rations allowed us, a half loaf with a small piece of meat, say one inch square, to each man for one day. A cool day, and without the least fire; and a great many of our men becoming sick and fast sinking from starvation, cold and want of clothing, having traded the last shoe and stocking from their feet to the guards to bribe them to procure some nourishment to keep them alive. Oh, if I could give you our sufferings in full! But I cannot without being challenged by you who read these lines, for I could not have believed it myself, but having tasted, seen and felt these things, I have to believe it is so.

Nov. 19. In the same prison. Allowed the same amount of rations above specified and of the same kind. A clear, cold day, and one of our men died on the lower floor, in an awful condition; starved and eat up by the army bug, far from home or friends, and his name unknown to me or any of us. He belonged to Kilpatrick's cavalry, and was captured during the raid made by him toward Richmond last month.

Nov. 20. In the same prison. Drew half a loaf of

shorts bread and one inch square of salt meat for one day's rations. To-day rather mild for winter weather. Some of the boys tried to escape and were captured and brought back, and bucked and gagged for one hour.

Nov. 21. Same prison. A very dull, rainy day. Drew bread and meat of the same kind, for this day's rations. Had roll-call for the first time in this prison, there being two hundred and forty-seven men on our floor this day.

Nov. 22. Same prison. Drew for this day's rations the same kind of bread and one inch square of sow-belly meat. A very nice day. It being Sunday. many of the Southern ladies and gentlemen can be seen passing by to a mill-race to see some folks dipped or christened, which ever you may call it.

Nov. 23. Same prison. Drew coarse bread and a small piece of meat for this day's rations. Made a smoking pipe out of clay from our rear prison-yard. Do not feel at all well.

Nov. 24. Same prison. Drew for this day's rations bread of the same kind and the small portion of meat allowed us. The sick all sent off from amongst us to the hospital. A very cool day.

Nov. 25. Same prison. A man of the 8th Michigan Cavalry died very suddenly on our floor last night. while drawing rations. Our rations were of bread and a small piece of beef, tasting good to our hungry and craving appetites.

Nov. 26. Same prison. Drew brown bread or

shorts and beef for this day's rations. A very nice day. Got our grub at 12 o'clock, A. M.

Nov. 27. Same prison. Drew the same amount and same kind of rations, and pretty hard at that. A cool, frosty day.

Nov. 28. Same prison. Drew the same brown bread and beef for this day's rations. A clear day all through. The lower floor sent up amongst us for doing some mischief unknown to me.

Nov. 29. Same prison. Drew brown bread and a little hog meat for this day's rations. Made coffee out of brown bread for dinner, by taking two bricks, placing them on the floor beside each other and getting a few splinters off the window and starting a fire in this way unknown to the guards—the first coffee made by me since my capture.

Nov. 30. Same prison. Drew the same allowance of rations and the same kind. Was searched by three rebel officers, and my spoon, knife, fork, inkstand and a watch, taken from me. My diary book was also taken, but my brother and brother-in-law's likenesses being in it, I got it and them back again by asking for them, but nothing else would they allow me or any of my brother soldiers to have.

Dec. 1. Danville Prison, No. 2. Drew brown bread—half of a five cent baker's loaf for one day's rations, with a small piece of meat, say one inch square. This is a fine day. A great many of us sick, and diseases of all kinds visiting our midst, carrying away scores of our number every day from these silent tombs of confinement; and I feel my whole system sinking under the ill-treatment of these inhuman beings.

Dec. 2. Same prison. Drew on this day our rations, brown bread and a small piece of beef. A clear day all through. The officer took down our names, company and regiment, in a book of record.

Dec. 3. Same prison. Drew brown bread and the same small allowance of meat. I might say to you for further information, that the brown bread so often spoken of is made out of cane-seed flour, termed brown bread by the soldiers on account of the dark color of it after being baked.

Dec. 4. Same prison. Drew brown bread and the same small piece of meat. Feel quite unwell myself, so weak and feeble I can scarcely stand, and from nothing else than hunger, and suffering from cold and sleeping on the bare, cold, rough and filthy floor of this prison.

Dec. 5. Same prison. Drew brown bread and the same allowance of beef for this day's rations. A fine day. Very sick, and feel myself sinking fast in this awful place of confinement, which I cannot make known to you in full, nor will I attempt it, but will leave these few lines with you for your consideration, and credit them as you may think for yourselves. But any and every thing set forth in this book I am willing to give a final account of to the great I Am, when pen and ink shall be no more with me, and I shall rest from all the fiery trials and hardships of this world, and cease from my labors for ever and ever.

Dec. 6. In the same prison. Drew the same brown bread and the same of meat for this day's rations. Sick myself, and very sick. A cool day. On this day the boys are undermining through the prison wall to try to make their and our escape from these dismal cells.

Dec. 7. In the same prison. Drew brown bread and beef for this day's rations. Still sick; clear and cold, freezing hard in the shade; and the boys still continuing their mining underneath the prison with the hope of escape in this way; but during the night they were detected and rushed up stairs, putting three floors on two, making it so much worse for us; and keeping us more strongly guarded than ever.

Dec. 8. In the same prison. Drew brown bread and beef, a small portion for this day's ration. A very cool day, freezing hard. Sent out to the rebel hospital from the prison, so weak that I could not stand, and twenty-eight more of my brother soldier inmates sent away in the same condition. I might describe to you in short, for I cannot in full reality without being challenged; but seeing and feeling it I have to believe it is so myself, that we were treated so hard on this day. The lieutenant and sergeant in charge of said prison came in this morning, and all that were not able to walk or stand up without help, were ordered out of doors of the prison to go to the hospital, and kept from this time in the morning out on the cold ground, exposed to the cold frosts of winter, until 2 o'clock in the afternoon, without fire or clothing of any kind to keep us warm, or anything to eat all this time, in this sick and weak state. God only knows our feelings at that trying moment—some praying that if it was only the Lord's will he would remove them by sudden death to their final resting place, and let them cease from the freezing and starvation and trials of this world in the jaws of the enemy or this inhuman people. Although not connected with any branch of the church, I am not an unbeliever, but acknowledge that there is a God, who formed all things and can make all things work together for our own and his good pleasure; and at this time did I well remember the kind promise given to us, that where one or two are assembled together in his name there would he be to bless them and do them good. And blessed be God and his great and adorable name, that he was with us at these trying moments, and did hear us, or at least some of us, while we were offering up our unhallowed petitions to him to release us from the jaws and hands of the enemy; and it is owing to his long-sparing mercy that I have been delivered from them and caused to meet my friends and little family and neighbors, with these few items set forth in the foregoing pages, to show you who may read of the trials and hardships we had to endure, and to exhibit God's mercies extended toward us in bringing us safely through them all; as he will all those who put their trust in him, and call upon his name in sincerity and in truth. Blessed be the name of the Lord of hosts, for good is he.

Dec. 9. In Danville Hospital, having arrived here last night at a late hour, almost frozen and in a very weak state, and put into our bunks without supper, and to do without breakfast. God only knows how we are to live, but I put my trust in him, that he will be a helper to me.

Dec. 10. In hospital. Sick, and very sick, and no hope of ever being any better, excepting God's merciful hand be extended toward me. A very cool day Drew one spoonful of hash, I cannot tell of what ingredients it was made of, and a small slice of brown bread for this day's rations. The rebels are changing the sick from one place to another; and Oh, if I could only give you a full account of the sudden deaths here, and of the most horrible sights you or I ever saw, or any one else on the face of the universe—nothing but skin and bone, having been brought down to a mere skeleton by these inhuman wretches.

Dec. 11. In the same hospital, No. 2. Three cases of smallpox have been removed out of our ward. Rations just the same, and hard at the best, but worse for us sick. Oh, if we had only the privilege of swill-tubs like our hogs at home, how happy would we feel to satisfy our almost gone appetites and bodies.

Dec. 12. Still in the same hospital. One man died in our ward this morning. Rations the same. A cool day all through. You can see the dead being removed at all hours in the day from this and surrounding hospitals.

Dec. 13. In the same prison of a hospital, in Ward 1, and First Division. Being Sunday; our rations the same. A very cool day. Feel very sick myself, and see a host of my brother soldiers in the same condition.

Dec. 14. In the same hospital, and no better. The rations the same—hard enough. A very cool day. No way of escape but to be content with our lot and put our trust in Him who ordereth all things well, and be resigned to our fate.

Dec. 15. In the same hospital; sitting up a little in bed, but no better. The rations the same daily—hard enough at all times.

Dec. 16. In the same hospital. Rations the same. Rice coffee this day, and corn bread and a small piece of meat.

Dec. 17. In the same hospital. A dull, cloudy, rainy day. Rations, rice coffee and corn bread for this day, with a small piece of meat and a living family trying to dissect it from the bone, which would cause any well person to cry out New York at the approach of it to their bedside.

Dec. 18. In the same hospital, and the rations the same as usual. A cool day; no better yet, and a great many cases of smallpox and yellow fever amongst us, causing death at the rate of fifty per day.

Dec. 19. Still in the same hospital. A clear cool day, and don't feel so well as I did a few days ago, and God only knows what is to become of us, as a suffering and starving people in these filthy and polluted cells of confinement.

Dec. 20. In the same hospital. Sunday; a cool, clear day all through. The rations the same as usual, and little and hard at that, I can assure you with a clear conscience of mind, which I am willing to give an account of when pen and ink will be with me no more, and I will be summoned to depart hence and be no more, but to meet that Judge who was with me through all of these trials and endurances.

Dec. 21. In the same hospital. A fine pleasant day. Rations the same daily, and many of us very ill in health, gradually growing weaker and sinking away by scores per day.

Dec. 22. Still in the same prison or hospital. Feel some better to-day. The grub the same—brown bread and a very small piece of bacon meat, and hard at that.

Dec. 23. In the same hospital. A nice cool day, and feel some better. Our rations the same as usual, and scant at that. I will state to you, that while in Uncle Sam's lines and at home, I got more at one meal than we get here in one week, and much better; so that you can judge for yourselves.

Dec. 24. In the same hospital. A clear cool day, and don't feel so well. Rations, corn bread and a small piece of meat. I will try to give you some idea of the material this corn bread was made of. In the first place, it consisted of corn tramped from the cob by horses, with cracked dirt and all, I can't say ground, for it was not, nor even allowed to be sifted before baking; it was baked without salt, by mixing it up as you would cow-feed at home, only allowing the batter to be made a little thicker, and then grabbing up as much as you could safely hold between your two hands and thrown into a pan and baked. When baked this was four men's allowance for twenty-four hours.

Dec. 25. In the same hospital, it being Christmas day. A warm nice day; the grub as usual, little enough. The rebel soldiers of this place fired thirteen rounds from their guns at the Arsenal place, as a salute for this day.

Dec. 26. In the same hospital. A cloudy, cool day. A man by the name of Fry, belonging to the 2d Ohio Cavalry, died in our ward, by being starved and frozen to death, and nothing else under the heavens. He was reduced to a mere skeleton before death.

Dec. 27. In the same hospital; a dull cloudy day. Rations as usual. Raining hard in the evening.

Dec. 28. In the same hospital. A very nice warm day, like spring weather at home. Feel a little better to-day. Our rations were the one-fourth of a corn loaf, as above described, for twenty-four hours, with a small piece of meat.

Dec. 27. In the same hospital. A fine clear day. Don't feel so well to-day. The rations as usual. A man by the name of Wellington of the 100th New York, died in our ward.

Dec. 30. In the same hospital; a clear warm day, and no better. The grub same as usual.

Dec. 31. In the same hospital; a wet rainy night. A very light breakfast, and no better. So ends this year, and no expectation from present appearances of getting better or being exchanged soon.

Jan. 1, 1864. Still in the same hospital. Very cold, clear and stormy day; feel a little better. Rations same, quarter of a corn loaf and a small piece of meat for one day.

Jan. 2. In the same hospital. A very cool day. The rations the same. Feel some little better.

Jan. 3. In the same hospital. A fine pleasant day, it being Sunday. Rations the same, and some better to-day. A great many dying off from amongst us with smallpox and yellow fever; you can see them carried to the dead-house from every ward and building, daily and hourly.

Jan. 4. In the same hospital. A cloudy day, but pleasant. Sent a letter through to our lines to my daughter Sarah E. Johnston, to let her know of my capture and whereabouts. Got permission to do so through the kindness of a rebel Colonel Mulfred, who had us in charge at the time.

Jan. 5. In the same hospital. A fine winter morning, cloudy all day. Feel some better; the grub as usual. After drawing a full suit of clothing, that had been sent us by the Sanitary Commission, we were ordered back to No. 6 prison to join our fellow soldiers and companions, and share the same old hard fate as before, by sleeping on this hard rough plank floor, and in the midst of filth of all kinds, which decency will not allow me to speak of in plain language.

Jan. 6. In No. 6 prison again. Snowed all day through. In an open, large brick building, without a window or fire in it, and not sufficient clothing to keep us from freezing. Snow from twelve to thirteen inches deep and still snowing.

Jan. 7. In the same prison. Drew five U. S. crackers for one day's rations, the first and only grub of Uncle Sam's since we fell into the hands of the Southern Confederacy. A snowy, cloudy day, and many of us sick and bad with smallpox, dying off very sudden, daily and hourly by scores, I might say at the rate of twenty or thirty a day.

Jan. 8. In the same No. 6 prison. A very cold

day. The rations corn bread and a small piece of meat, and Oh heavens, what stuff to present to men to eat; it would cause the dogs at home to turn away in disgust if offered to them, yet we are compelled to eat it or starve, when offered to us in these sick and weak hours when life seems hardly visible.

Jan. 9. A clear cold day. Drew four ounces of beef and corn bread for this day's rations. The amount of bread for this and similar days allowed us is the half of a loaf for twenty-four hours, being mixed up like slops or swill at home for cattle, without salt or anything added thereto, only made thicker than what we would call slop or swill; just what a man could grab up with his hands by folding them together, and baked in like manner, and presented to us daily from this time on for our food; and the God of Heaven only knows what stuff it is to be fed on, when we often could not eat it, and would throw it out of the window, and their hogs and chickens coming along would pick and smell over it and then turn away with scorning to eat it. So you who read these few lines can imagine for yourselves, and us in a starved and dying condition, our appetites having forsaken us at times altogether, and our stomachs become so weak that they refused to digest this coarse dirty food, too fine ground for cracked hominy and too coarse ground to be called Indian corn meal, and never allowed to pass through a seive before being baked, with all the contents that rats and mice often leave in corn, the silk and husks all baked together, and often not baked at all, but burned outside and nothing but batter inside.

Jan. 10. Still in the same No. 6 prison, situated in Danville, on the bank of the Dan river, 140 miles from Richmond, in Pittslin county, due south-west from Richmond, Va. A clear cold day; drew the same small amount of rations and the same as described in the former pages. I have become so weak and nervous from the want of necessary food and treatment like human beings, you will please excuse me from enumerating the amount allowed us and the materials composed of, as I have given you some insight of what they were as near as I can, for God only knows some of the ingredients that they consisted of, for I don't, nor none of my brother soldiers could have any knowledge of them.

Jan. 11. In the same prison, and a cool day. Smallpox, fevers of various kinds, scurvy, chronic diarrhœa, and many other diseases, are thinning our ranks by scores per day.

Jan. 12. In the same prison. A very cool day. The rations the same, corn bread and a small piece of meat, and hard stuff at that, I can assure you, for us sick to attempt to eat.

Jan. 13. A dull rainy day, and in the same prison. Drew corn bread and the shanks of shoulders and hams of old speck, with the rinds cut off before offered to us, cooked altogether and given to us in like manner, and you might eat it or let it alone.

Jan. 14. In the same prison; a clear spring-like day. Rations the same, corn bread and salt meat, and the same amount, very small; and Oh if we could only eat it, but our weak stomachs and sick bodies refuse to crave such diet any longer, and God only knows what is to become of us as a suffering people.

Jan. 15. A most beautiful day, and in the same prison. Drew for this day the same kind of rations, corn bread and salt meat, and some cabbage leaves and stocks boiled in the water of the meat, and allowed say one of our tea-cups full of said mixture for this day.

Jan. 16. A clear, warm day; in the same prison. Still wasting away and becoming weaker, and fed daily on the same kind of rations.

Jan. 17. In the same prison, and still drawing corn bread and a small piece of meat for our day's rations, that our dogs or swine at home would scorn to eat.

Jan. 18. A cloudy, rainy morning; in the same prison. Drew the same kind of rations for this day as heretofore; and Oh, if I had but one crumb or crust of wheat bread to feed my gnawing and weak appetite, for must I die in want of it? For I can see them daily dying for want of it, as well as myself; and death seems to be to each one of us inevitably our doom, unless God so orders, by his kind will, our delivery from out of the jaws of the enemy. This is our only hope of rescue.

Jan. 19. Still in the same prison. A fine, clear, cool day. Drew corn bread and a little piece of meat for this day, say never more than one inch square of meat for one day's rations.

Jan. 20. A fine, clear, cold day, and in the same prison. The rations as usual this day. To-day makes four months confined in these hellish places of confinement, and treated worse than hogs; shut up closer, and not allowed to go out to the rear only six at a time, out of nine hundred, and wait their return before six more can go; and you can imagine our condition, with chronic diarrhœa raging amongst us, which decency will not allow me to explain to the public. We never had our cells or rooms washed out, or even a change of clothing, for those four months, and we were compelled to stand, lie down or sleep in the same filth, with a living family to annoy us day and night; and I have known men to lose every hair of their head, and be as bald as though they had been born without any, from this living family above spoken of becoming so numerous that they could not rid themselves of them till the work was done. Now, ladies and gentlemen, hearing and seeing, by the old adage, is said to be believing; but I will tell you what I think—both these and feeling and tasting, I think should be the naked truth, and your writer has, and will as long as he lives, feel them.

Jan. 21. A clear, cool day; in the same prison. The rations kept back from us this day on account of the third floor tearing up the garret floor to make fire to keep them and us on the second floor from freezing; and the only way we had to have fire after obtaining it in this way, was to lay two of our brick pillows together and then make some fine splints and set them on fire, and lay them on the bricks to keep it from burning the floor or setting the building on fire; and then gather around this fire in a ring to keep the light or smoke being discovered by the rebel sentinels or officers, or we would be deprived even of this privilege. So for this one offense from this third floor the whole house had to do forty-eight hours without one morsel of food to eat.

Jan. 22. In the same prison. Drew corn bread and meat for this day's ration, and hellish at that. Before going any further, I might be asked to inform the reader how we managed to get a knife or fork to eat with, or to split kindlings for fire, as we had been searched heretofore and all these things taken from us. Now, if you will call on the writer, he will show and prove to you that cold, hunger and starvation is the mother of all inventions, as he has in his possession a knife, a fork and two spoons, and a smoking pipe, made by him in this prison and safely brought through the lines by him.

Jan. 23. A fine cool day. In the same prison. Drew half a loaf of corn bread and cabbage slop. Oh, to be offered such stuff to eat, when the animal family would sink under such treatment, and we to be content with our lot.

Jan. 24. A cool, clear day. Drew corn bread and a small piece of meat, and cabbage runts, and the rotten outside leaves cooked in the broth of the meat, worms, dirt and all together; hard stuff to feed men or prisoners on.

Jan. 25. A fine cool day. Rations the same, only on this day, owing to too many rotten and outside leaves of cabbage being kept on hands until they became so wilted as to lose almost taste, they issued them to us in a raw state; two wagon loads of such stuff amongst nine hundred men.

Jan. 26. A fine clear day. Drew the same kind of rations for this day. In the same prison.

Jan. 27. A fine clear day. Drew corn bread and salt meat for this day's rations, and four spoonfuls of vinegar to each man.

Jan. 28. A fine clear day. Drew corn bread and salt meat and bean soup, with two beans to one gallon of water, and not good at that.

Jan. 29. A clear warm day. Rations the same. The lower floor fired into by two of the rebel sentinels, the balls passing in at one door and going out at the other, wounding two of our men pretty badly and others making narrow escapes.

Jan. 30. In prison yet, and a warm nice day. Drew half a loaf of corn bread and a small piece of salt meat for this day's ration.

Jan. 31. In the same prison. A fine warm day. looks like spring outside, but not so pleasant with us. Shut up in these filthy cells, everything looks gloomy, and no chance for release or escape from the jaws and hands of these hardened wretches.

Feb. 1. Still in the same prison. A wet, foggy and rainy day. The lower floor driven up to our second floor on account of undermining the prison and underground one hundred and seventy-five yards, to get outside of the sentinels to make their and our escape: but on account of sixty-five men making their escape the others seeing them release themselves, crowded into this small drift or channel, almost suffocating themselves, and in trying to get some of them to keep back and go in regular order, they were overheard by the guard or sentinel and forced up stairs, making it much worse for us all; and we were more strongly guarded and used much worse from this on, and God only knows it was bad enough before this; and putting nine hundred men on two floors, in place of three, you can imagine for yourselves our crowded condition, and so many sick among us in such a filthy and polluted place of confinement, which I cannot make known to you in full.

Feb. 2. In the same prison. Very sick, not able to help myself in the least on account of a severe attack of bilious colic, my appetite having become so delicate that I cannot eat the corn bread allowed me; my small portion of meat is all that I can eat, and it is now my sole dependence for food to save my life, fast wasting away by the barbarous treatment of these inhuman beings.

Feb. 3. In the same prison. Drew rations on this day for the first time for three days, as you can see that two days previous to this the rations were ordered to be kept from us on account of violating their rules in digging out and trying to make our escape from them. The commissary of rations, after keeping our rations from us those three days, said they might as well let us have them again, for we were the d——st Yanks he ever saw, for we could ground-hog out of any place; and to tell you the honest truth, this channel was executed by the use of old bones as a pick to loosen the earth, which was carried back in our hats or caps, and a small box underneath the lower floor, and packed closely so no detection could or would be noticed until finished and our escape made, which would have been the case if the boys had gone in regularly about every five minutes, as they promised they would before making the attempt. All who were able would have been released at that time and in this way. But Oh, how soon can all our hopes be made sad unto us.

Feb. 4. In the same prison. So ill, and nothing to eat, or at least that I could. But for the necessity of saving my life a little longer, I had to trade my shoes off to one of our own men for fourteen dollars of our greenbacks, and with these means I managed to get a loaf of wheat bread sent in to me by a good Union man of this town, and this I made do me three weeks for food, and a small loaf at that; and from being compelled to dispose of my shoes you will see the result, by having to pass to the rear through the mud of the yard, in my bare feet, and it a cool day at this season of the year.

Feb. 5. In the same prison. On this day had another severe attack of bilious colic from having to go barefooted to get food to save my life—and I could not have lasted but a few moments under the pain and sufferings, if not relieved by the skill of one of our own men administering salt-water to me for a vomit, and red peppers smashed in water applied to my feet and stomach and taken inwardly, to get up perspiration; and in so doing saved my life, to appear here before you in these pages, giving you all the light I can on the barbarities and treatment while in those prisons; and as a memento of my kind and generous friend in time of need—and a friend was he indeed to me—his name is Nelson H. Cole, of the 112th Illinois regiment. God bless him.

Feb. 6. In the same prison. No better yet. Drew corn bread and salt meat, and as I cannot eat my corn bread, I am compelled to trade my bread rations to my friend and messmate, B. P. Brubaker, for the small portion of salt meat allowed him, and to live on these and the loaf of bread before spoken off, and thankful that it is God's will to furnish me thus and save my life from a starving and gnawing condition. This is a cloudy day all through.

Feb. 7. In the same prison yet. A cloudy, cool day. Drew corn bread and little-hog meat for this day's rations. Now, gentlemen and ladies, if you wish me to explain to you how this got "little-hog meat" for its name, just call at my house, or on me or any of my family, and they or I can show you a specimen of the ribs taken out of this so-termed little-hog meat, and kept concealed and fetched through to our lines, for a sample to you or any of you who wish to see them.

Feb. 8. In the same prison. A fine clear day. Drew corn bread and little-hog meat for this day's rations. A great many sick and dying daily from amongst us, and I can see starvation and death staring us in the face—others having fulfilled their appointed time here on earth, and not knowing how soon we may be summoned to follow their footsteps and rest from the trials of this world and cease from all our labors.

Feb. 9. Still in the same prison. A cloudy, cool day. Drew corn bread and little-hog meat for this day's rations, with the small allowance of say half a pint of the water the meat was cooked in to each man, as a substitute for coffee or tea, to drink while eating, for we never have seen coffee or tea since it was our misfortune to be captured and fall into these inhuman beings' hands.

Feb. 10. In the same prison. A clear cool day. Drew corn and wheat bread mixed for this day's rations, and the same for drink as above spoken of, and little-hog meat as usual. Now, ladies and gentlemen, I don't want you to think that I am presenting these pages here before you who may think worth while reading them, for the purpose of casting any slur upon the South further than they are deserving of it, nor can I give it to you in reality or in full without being challenged; but since my return home I have been asked by my best friends, relations and neighbors, how I was treated, and what I got to eat; and I have told them that it was a question that I could not answer them—that I never could nor never would tell any one in full, for I would not be believed —nor could I have believed my best and truest friends had they told me in full, without doubting. But, gentlemen and ladies, one thing I can tell you—I have seen these hard trials, and tasted and felt of them, and will feel them till the number of my days are ended on earth, and the summons of death bids me depart from the trials of this world and enter the next and far better one, when I am willing to give an account to the great I Am, if this be not a true copy, to the best of my knowledge and ability, here presented to you.

Feb. 11. In the same prison. A clear cool day. Drew corn and wheat bread mixed, and little-hog meat, and the same for drink as above spoken of, for this day's rations; and it is owing to God's merciful hand extended to us that we are permitted to keep this record for you, for we can see death staring us in the face, while numbers are daily removed from our midst from starvation and ill-treatment, which you could not believe your writer, nor any one else, if they or I were to give you in full. But having come through those awful trials and feelings of starving, I have to believe it is so; and will leave these lines with you for your consideration.

Feb. 12. Still in the same prison. A clear, cool day. Drew corn bread and little-hog meat for this day's rations, and hard at that, I can assure you.

Feb. 13. Still in the same prison. A clear, cool day, and very sick on this day, and many of my poor brother soldiers likewise, and our appetites refuse to receive this hard and small portion of unhealthy food allowed us.

Feb. 14. Still in the same prison. A clear, cool day. The same rations of corn bread and little hog meat as heretofore, with the water after the meat has been cooked in it allowed us for drink; and I can feel myself sinking fast, now almost reduced to a skeleton, and not me alone, but thousands of others sharing the same hard fate. God only knows what is to become of us, if not soon released from the jaws and hands of these our enemies.

Feb. 15. In the same prison. Drew corn bread and old speck meat for this day's rations. Snowed all this day, and us in a house the windows of which are without glass, and no fire allowed us at all, and almost clotheless; and to lie all the time on a damp, rough floor, and in this feeble state reduced so one can hardly help the other. Just pause and consider for yourselves, and see the situation now presented to you.

Feb. 16. Still in the same prison. A cloudy, cool day, and no better, still knowing myself to become weaker, and can see hundreds of others by my side in the same condition.

Feb. 17. A cloudy, cool day. In the same prison. On this day the rebels having us in charge gave us two stoves to each floor, or to three hundred of us, with the allowance of one bushel of coal for twenty-four hours to each floor, and the stoves were like the first I ever saw, old-fashioned metal ones, without even a place to remove the ashes from, and the coal not good, it would burn for a short while and then die out and become like lime before slacked; we would then have to throw down the stove to get it cleaned out for a new fire. So in a few days these self-heaters got played out with Uncle Sam's boys, and we rolled them out of our way, and did without fire from this time on, with only the assistance of a fire now and then brought in by the two bricks we used for our pillows and the few splinters spoken of before. You will observe that they did not furnish us with these stoves because they would afford us any comfort, or from any good feeling they had toward us, but for the mere purpose of saving their building from bring stripped by us to get the splinters that we formerly had been using to make the small fires on the brick pillows, or I might say that we used for a chair to sit on, a table to eat off, and a cupboard or dresser to lay our food on, for this was our only piece of furniture in the building, and we had to apply it to a great many uses; and it was often taken from us and thrown away; and the only way we could succeed in getting another would be to pry it out of the wall of the building. On this day we drew the same small allowance of corn and cane-seed, ground in flour, and then baked into a kind of bread for us, with the ounce of meat for twenty-four hours.

Feb. 18. A cloudy morning, and still in the same prison. Drew on this day the same kind of bread and the same of meat, with the addition of what they called bean soup. If I had had the chance of naming it I would have called it bug or worm soup, for it swam thick on top with them out of the beans, such as you have often seen in our old peas at home.

Feb. 19. A fine clear day. Drew old pork and sourkrout with our bread for this day's rations,— an extra dish for us, and I can assure you that we went into it with all our muscles, having been in these prisons five months, and I am safe in saying to you, starved all this time. I never can or will tell you who read these pages, in full our hard lot and treatment, for I could not have believed my best friend, had I not seen, tasted and felt it myself, and will as long as I live.

Feb. 20. A clear, fine day. Still in the same prison. Drew the same kind of rations as the day previous—God knows hard enough; but we have to be thankful that we are allowed such.

Feb. 21. A fine clear day. In the same prison.

Drew brown bread and one ounce of little-hog meat for twenty-four hours' rations.

Feb. 22. A cloudy day. In the same prison yet. Drew the same of bread and meat, and also three spoonfuls of vinegar allowed to each man, and I can assure you we thought it a treat.

Feb. 23. A fine clear day. In the same prison. Drew brown bread; that you may understand me when I say brown bread, it is baked out of chopped corn and the meal of cane-seed, put together with water, without salt or anything else added thereto; and also little-hog meat, and what they called rice soup, but I must say rotten soup, for we could not eat it, and when thrown out of the window their hogs and chickens, after an inspection of it, would turn away from it with contempt, refusing to eat what a human family had to live on daily. Only think!

Feb. 24. A most beautiful, clear day. Drew on this day corn bread and the refuse of old rusty bacon and the same so-called rice soup, for this day's rations.

Feb. 25. A clear, fine day. Drew corn bread, little-hog meat and bean soup, and poor at that, also a ration of wood, two sticks one and a half inch square and two feet long, for three days' fuel, only to keep us from burning the house down, not from any love for us or any good feeling toward us, but simply because they could not help themselves.

Feb. 26. A clear, cool day. Drew the same kind of rations and the same amount. There were four fights last night among our men on account of raids made upon their food. Their hunger becoming so great, they have commenced to steal from one another; and while I am writing there are two more fights among the boys.

Feb. 27. Still in Danville prison, No. 6. On this day drew corn bread, little-hog meat and three spoonfulls of sourkrout to each man for this day's rations. I feel very sick, and Oh to look around me in this place and see death working amongst our fast wasting frames, calling many from our midst just for the want of food or nourishment that we can eat.

Feb. 28. A fine, clear day. In the same prison. Drew for this day's rations brown bread, little-hog meat and bean soup—the beans something similar to our old peas at home, and when boiled neither you nor I could say but it was meat and bean soup both, from the hides afloat upon the broth from the living family the so-called beans contained before being cooked.

Feb. 29. A fine, warm day. Drew on this day for rations corn bread, little-hog meat and rice soup, the rice being thrown into large iron kettles, set in a furnace, something similar to those for boiling sugar at home, and boiled in like manner, without salt or anything else but the rice and water, and the kettles never washed out for all this time of cooking since the war began—for as soon as emptied more water was thrown in and another mixture made, often worse than any swill or slop for the swine at home.

March 1. A wet, cloudy, cool morning, and still in the same prison. Drew for this day's rations corn bread, little-hog meat and rice soup.

March 2. A fine, clear day. In the same prison.

Drew for this day's rations corn bread and little-hog meat.

March 3. A fine, clear day. Drew for this day's rations corn bread, little-hog meat and rice soup.

March 4. A fine spring day. Drew for rations on this day corn bread, little-hog meat and rice boiled in the water of this, and when cooked thinned down with cold water—and of all the stuff to be afterwards called rice soup!

March 5. A fine, clear day. Drew corn bread, little-hog meat and the above described rice soup.

March 6. Still in the same prison. Drew for this day's rations corn bread, little-hog meat and rice soup—three parts of a pint of this miserable stuff to each man.

March 7. A fine, clear day. In the same prison. Drew corn bread, little-hog meat, and bean soup made of black beans, well known by us boys termed negro beans—a table spoonful of beans to three parts of a pint of water allowed to each man.

March 8. A fine, clear day. Drew for this day's rations corn bread, old bacon meat and bean soup, and hellish at that. This is a hard termed word, ladies and gentlemen; but you must excuse me for breaking out in such language, as I cannot help it, when presented with such diet as our hogs would scorn to eat.

March 9. A fine, clear day. Drew wheat bread and fine little-hog meat, or at least we thought it very nice; but anything is a good sauce to a hungry and starving appetite, I can assure you.

March 10. A wet, rainy day. Drew good wheat

bread, but a small portion of it, little-hog meat and bean soup, for this day's rations.

March 11. A cloudy day, and raining. Drew wheat bread, and good enough if there was only enough of it; little-hog meat and black bean soup for this day's rations.

March 12. A clear, cool day. On this day drew corn bread, pea soup and little-hog meat.

March 13. A clear, cool day. Drew corn bread, little-hog meat and black bean soup for this day's rations.

March 14. Still in the same prison. A clear day. Drew corn bread, little-hog meat and black beans, a spoonful to each man, for this day's rations.

March 15. A cloudy, dull day. Got word from my oldest daughter, the first word from home since my capture; got it through a letter from Susan Catharine Brubaker to Benjamin P. Brubaker, her husband, a messmate of mine in this solitary place of confinement, and a member of my company, who was captured at the same time and place that I was; and Oh, if any of you could only know the joy and comfort that these few words from home gave us! Drew on this day corn bread and a mixture of meat, black beans, corned beef and little-hog meat. You may imagine from the enumeration of the above drawing of rations that we had received a large supply; I can state the amount in full in a very short way, when I tell you that I could hold all of my share in one hand and then not full—and for hard stuff I need not tell you, for you could not believe it was so, but my God be the judge for me if I am not presenting you a true copy of what I have felt, tasted and endured, and not me alone, but thousands of others shared the same fate; and how we have lived and come through it all I cannot say--but it seems to me that nothing else but a kind Providential hand has done it all.

March 16. A cloudy, cool day. Drew corn bread old speck meat and black bean soup for this day's rations.

March 17. Still in the same prison. A fine, cool day. Drew corn bread, no meat, and brown bean soup for this day.

March 18. A fine spring day. Drew corn bread and some pretty good salt pork for this day, but a very small piece of it.

March 19. A fine, clear day. In the same prison. Drew corn bread, little-hog meat and black bean soup, for this day, and nothing but corn from this time on; if it had only been good we would have felt satisfied.

March 20. A clear, cool day. Drew corn bread, little-hog meat and brown and white bean soup for this day's rations. Still in the same prison.

March 21. A cool, raw day. Drew corn bread and little-hog meat, and little at that, I can say with safety.

March 22. A cool, snowy day all through. Drew corn bread, little-hog meat and black bean soup; and by a box being sent from home to a brother inmate soldier of mine, and he being a good friend, although no relation, he gave me a drawing of tea, and I can tell you it was the best I ever tasted, or at least it seemed so to me at this time and place, as this was my first taste of tea from the time of my capture up to this day.

March 23. Snow on this day twelve inches deep, and a fine winter day. Drew corn bread and rice soup, but no meat, for this day's rations.

March 24. Still in the same prison. A fine, clear day, and the snow melting away fast. On this day drew corn bread, speck meat and rice soup.

March 25. A soft, rainy day. Drew corn bread and rice soup, but no meat, for this day's rations.

March 26. Drew corn bread and rice soup, not so good as you or I feed our hogs with at home. A clear day. Preaching in the prison at 5 o'clock in the evening, for the first time; you can find the text in the 3d chapter of St. John, 3d and 4th verse.

March 26. A clear day. Drew for this day's rations corn bread and rice soup that we could not eat, it was so bad. Oh if I could only have got a sample of it through the lines with me, I might have showed you perhaps more than you ever saw or ever will—at least it is my earnest desire that no one will ever be so unfortunate as to see what I have seen, of which I am not able ever to make known unto you in full without being challenged, nor will I attempt it.

March 27. This is Easter Sunday at home and many other places, and a very nice, clear day; but not so with us here in our dismal and solitary place of confinement, deprived of all the dainties and luxuries of life gotten up on such days, and our weary heads and sickened bodies having no place to lie down on but a rough plank floor, without clothing of any kind except what was on us, and in this cold month of winter without fire at any time. You, my kind reader, may think how can this be so, and you and they endure it all? Yes, I might as well say so too; but having both seen, tasted and felt of this bitter cup of trial, I have to believe it to be so, and have just to say, thank God and him alone for his mercy in bringing me and others safely through them all.

March 28. A cloudy, warm day. Drew rice soup and old speck meat for this day's rations. You who may read these few pages, and see that we daily receive the same kind of diet, or almost so, and seeing rice soup and bean soup mentioned so often, may think we were not so badly treated after all; but will you please consider how it was made, or of what it consisted. Well, it was made of the water off of whatever kind of meat was cooked for us, no difference how old or how salty it might be; the beans or rice thrown into it in big iron kettles set in a furnace, and never cleaned out from the time the war began, and just taken out and given to us and filled up again in like manner, and you can imagine for yourselves what kind of soup it would be.

March 29. A cloudy, dull and rainy morning; thundered and lightened very hard all forenoon, and at 12 o'clock the rain became so heavy as to overflow every nook or low piece of ground through this town of Danville, nine miles from the line of North Carolina, Pittslin county; and the guards having returned, or sought shelter in a small building across a run or small ditch, were in a short time taken by surprise, having been turned out by the building upsetting, and guns and men and all passing down the stream some distance before they could be rescued, losing their guns and accoutrements.

March 30. A nice, warm day, but a gloomy one to me, suffering from the diseases of imprisonment; God only knows the awful suffering I am enduring this day, away from home, and no friends to console me, with the exception of my brother soldiers, and they or the most of them are in the same condition, and I cannot expect any relief from them.

April 1. A very cool day. Through the influence of our ward-master we were removed to the rebel hospital, one mile further up in the before mentioned town; and there, stripped of what few rags there were on us, and as naked as the day we were born, we were placed between two muslin sheets, in a room without fire, on a straw bed for the first time while in the hands of these inhuman beings, and without supper or anything to eat from the day before; although my appetite did not crave any food, it appeared hard that we were not allowed the privilege of seeing some.

April 2. Got no breakfast until 2 o'clock in the afternoon, and then drew five ounces of wheat bread and a small piece of salt pork for two meals, and had to eat it raw, with a small cup of coffee made out of browned rice. A fine, clear day all through.

April 3. In Hospital No. 1, ward A. A very wet day, and all night through very cool. Drew corn bread, and the same kind of meat and rice soup.

April 4. So sick this morning that I cannot sit up at all; a cloudy, wet day. On what they call weak diet; God knows it always has been weakening enough to us all. Drew wheat bread and rice soup for this day's rations.

April 5. A cloudy, cool day. Not any better: scores dying in our midst from smallpox, starvation and ill-treatment; drew wheat bread and a small piece of meat, and I can assure you, it was a small piece indeed to look at, let alone to live on.

April 6. A fine, clear day. Drew for this day's rations potato bread mixed with a little corn, and tea made out of what I will never tell you, for I do not know myself; not any better and still becoming weaker.

April 7. On this day had our old rags brought back to us again, with the name of being washed, and had the privilege of dressing with them again; drew rations of bread made like wheat bread, and hard at that.

April 8. A clear, fine day. Drew meat and potatoes and bread of the same. Am very sick to-day.

April 9. A wet, cool day. Allowed to eat three times to-day, because they well know we cannot eat at all. If done to torment us I cannot tell; let God be their and my judge.

April 10. A fine spring day, and had three meals of the same kind of food.

April 11. A nice day, and moved down from No. 1 to No. 3 Division Hospital. Drew hard tack sent through from our lines to us by the Sanitary Commission—two crackers to each patient. This having been a hospital for smallpox patients. I saw with my own eyes men moved out to the cold ground and left to lie and suffer in this condition from early in the morning till late at night, when they were thrown into a large wagon and hauled away to some unknown spot out of view, like loads of wood, or in as careless a manner as we would do that work at home.

April 12. A fine day. The same grub, only bread in place of hard tack. Great excitement among our men on seeing cars moving into this town all day, with the report that we were to be sent through for parole from this place to Richmond.

April 13. Mark the sad disappointment to us unfortunate beings! How soon all things can be made to us sad in the most bright and hopeful hours! On this day seven hundred of our men were placed in the cars, out of No. 6 prison, and taken just the reverse road from that which they were informed the day before they were to be sent by the rebels—right from the smoke, we might say, into the fire. Sent to Andersonville prison, Georgia, where but very few have survived to tell the tale of the awful death their comrades had to die; yes, they had to die—they could not live under such treatment.

April 14. A fine, clear day. Orders came to our hospital that all who were able to walk back on this day to the prisons from whence they came, would be sent through to our lines for exchange. Although feeble and weak indeed, I thought I would make the attempt to get back, so I might get through and live, for I must soon die if left here much longer, but in my effort to reach the door of the hospital I fainted and fell, and became insensible to every thing. So I was taken back to bed, and well for me, as you will see: it was only to get us in good heart so they could send us off to Georgia, to the slaughter-pen of Andersonville prison; and this is all that saved me, for those that were taken with me and sent there never returned, but are numbered among the dead.

April 15. A fine day. Drew salt meat, corn bread and tea. This day the men in No. 3 prison were removed to Andersonville prison, and you can see that all that were able to get back to their prisons were sent along. And when I was trying to get back, thinking it would be better for me, God in his kind providence saw it was not, and said, You can't go.

April 16. A fine day. Drew mush for this day, with molasses, and one biscuit.

April 17. A fine day. Drew corn bread, salt meat and pickled onions for this day. Feel very sick.

April 18. A fine day. Feel somewhat better; drew the same grub, without the onions.

April 19. A very nice day. Drew on this day corn bread, salt meat, tea, and a small portion of rice.

April 20. A very fine day. Was sent away from this Hospital No. 3, ward A, at 8 o'clock in the morning, for Richmond, Va.; came forty-two miles to a washed away bridge across a creek, named Barren Bottoms, and changed cars there, the rebel lieutenant having us in charge saying to the boys. One thing I can assure you, that you are going to Richmond, for I am to deliver you up there; but what will become of you afterwards I cannot tell, but hope you may all get along well. This was the first and only good feeling man to us in the Rebel Confederacy. We arrived in Richmond at 10 o'clock at night, making a march of 140 miles.

April 21. Here is from out of the smoke into the fire; here we have again to enter into a building or hospital, which has been used since the war began for the relief of wounded men, with amputations, not one able to help the other, and I can never think there was a change of clothing put thereon; and inhabited by a living family to annoy you day and night. No artist can paint nor human tongue describe in full to you the awful condition of the building in which we were placed.

April 22. Here you will find me amongst others sent back to Richmond, and suffering under the greatest agony and pains of life that mortal man can be placed in under such circumstances; and though in this feeble state, rice, corn bread, and coffee made out of browned rice, is our only diet; and Oh, if only got up right, we could relish it.

April 23. A fine day. Drew a spoonful of vinegar, rice, corn bread and a small piece of beef.

April 24. A cloudy day. Rations the same; a dreary day to me and others in such weak and feeble state of health, and no hope before us but death, and then the grave.

April 25. A fine day. Rations the same, only no vinegar, and my health growing worse.

April 26. A fine, clear, warm day. A blind man died instantly in our ward; he lost his sight from the effects of smallpox, and no care taken of him.

April 27. Some better. A fine day; drew rations as usual; a man died in our ward.

April 28. A fine, clear day. Drew rations as usual. Not so well as yesterday.

April 29. A fine day. Paroled on this day; drew corn bread and rice; feel quite sick and feeble; not able to help myself in the least.

April 30. Leaving Richmond to come to City Point for exchange; left the city at 8 o'clock in the morning, and arrived at City Point at 2 o'clock in the afternoon, a march by water of 62 miles.

May 1. Left City Point at 10 o'clock in the forenoon, and at 3 o'clock in the afternoon arrived at Fortress Monroe, a distance by water of 80 miles.

May 2. Left Fortress Monroe at 11 o'clock at night, arriving at Annapolis, Md., on the 3d of May, one hundred and fifty miles by water, and it seemed to me as though I had been released out of purgatory and got to heaven—our own land, country and government, and the best ever upon the face of the earth. I might mention, too, that I was brought through to our lines on what is called a tug steamer, and then placed on the fine steamer "New York," and brought with six hundred other as helpless beings as myself, not one able to help the other; and the change was so great that I lost all control of myself—my senses gave way, and I was carried off the boat on stretchers and placed in bed, and when I revived, I felt as though wakened out of a fine sleep, I could not believe that I was amongst living people.

May 3. Arrived in Annapolis, Md., at 11 o'clock;

was washed, and drew new drawers and shirt, and put in bed, very sick. A cool day; rained all night.

May 4. A fine, clear day; in a pleasant place and all nice around me, with the very best of diet, and well attended.

May 5. A fine day, and drew a new suit from Uncle Sam, and the best of care for our comfort and welfare.

May 6. A fine day; feel some better. Diet can't be beat for good, and the women and men come in so kindly to see us.

May 7. A fine day, and still improving. A fresh change of clothing from the hospital. A committee of twelve women and men came all the way from Philadelphia to see our lamentable condition from starvation and ill-treatment while in the jaws of the enemy.

May 8. A fine day; some better. Diet good, can't be beat; and all the attendance a sick or wounded soldier could wish for.

May 9. A fine, clear and warm day, cloudy in the evening and rained.

May 10. A fine day; four hundred more sick and paroled prisoners came again on the steamer "New York" to Annapolis.

May 11. A nice day, till evening; rained all night. Feel some better, am just able to sit up in bed and take a distant view of the bay's beauty, with the steamers. the sail boats, and the birds and water fowls making their horizontal circles over the briny deep.

May 12. A nice day. Inspected, and a great many old patients sent off to their commands.

May 13. A wet, rainy day. My feet are badly swollen; don't feel near so well. Do think this is one of the best fitted up places in the world for sick or wounded soldiers; there is nothing wanting or kept back, but every thing done to make him think he will and must get well. I just tell you Uncle Sam has a very large family, but he is rich; and he is not only rich, but he is kind to those that were true to him. Will you mind that, all you who read these lines.

May 14. A wet day all through. Feel a little better.

May 15. A nice day. Transfered from ward A to ward B, division No. 1, section No. 2, and room 8.

May 16. A very nice day. Feel some better. On light diet. A man died in the next room.

May 17. A clear day, and everything most beautiful. The sergeant in charge sent after me to know the date of Postley damning us so in Richmond Hospital on the 27th of April, or thereabouts, not sooner.

May 18. A very nice day. Don't feel so well.

May 19. A fine day. In bed all day, sick.

May 20. Rained all night. In bed all day, and feel a great deal worse, having taken cold.

May 21. A fine day. Mr. Postley came to see me concerning his son, who is arrested and under trial for life.

May 22. A fine day. Feel some better.

May 23. A fine day. Feel a great deal worse.

May 24. A wet, rainy day. No better; suffering a great deal.

May 25. A nice day, and no better.

May 26. A very nice day, and suffering from another severe attack of bilious colic.

May 27. A nice day, and very sick.

May 28. A fine day. In a great deal of pain and misery.

May 29. A fine day. Feel much better again. General inspection in our ward.

May 30. A fine day, and still improving.

May 31. A fine day, and able to sit up a little.

June 1. A nice day, and still getting better.

June 2. A fine day, and able to go down stairs again.

June 3. A fine day. I am able to write and walk about again, and feel pretty well.

June 4. A fine, clear day. Was taken up to Doctor Ealy's office, and from there out in an ambulance to Parole Camp, four miles, in behalf of a young man by the name of Postley, arrested on a charge of being disloyal to his country. Got back to my quarters at 12 o'clock.

June 5. A fine day. Inspected to be sent away. Am still improving in health.

June 6. A fine, clear day; stormed in the evening. Had orders to be ready at 1 o'clock to be shipped to Annapolis Junction, Md., but for some reason was not sent.

June 7. A very nice day. Left Annapolis at 8 o'clock and came to Annapolis Junction, making a distance of 20 miles.

June 8. A fine, clear day. Don't feel so well.

June 9. A wet, rainy morning; cleared up at 10 o'clock—a fine day. Feel pretty well.

June 10. A fine, pleasant day. Feel pretty well. Allowed twenty ounces of ale per day.

June 11. A fine day all through. Don't feel quite so well. Helped the ward master to draw clothing.

June 12. A fine day. Feel a great deal better. Went to preaching in the grove close by, and the text can be found in the 6th chapter of John, 47th verse— the first opportunity I have had of going to church for twelve months.

June 13. A fine morning. Drew a fatigue coat Feel some better; went to the store at the Junction for the first time.

June 14. A fine day. Saw and helped to amputate the arm of Alexander Wallace, of Co. B, First Michigan regiment of sharpshooters. Drew seven pairs of slippers. Am improving in health as fast as can be expected.

June 15. A fine day. Still improving in health, my disease chronic diarrhœa and scurvy, with swelled feet.

June 16. A fine day. Feel a great deal better.

June 17. An extremely hot day. Don't feel near so well.

June 18. A fine, clear day. Just able to walk around a little to-day.

June 19. A fine day, and have preaching in the grove close by. The cars of two trains ran into each other, smashing them badly. Three men seriously hurt and a great deal of stock injured.

June 20. A fine, clear day. All paroled prisoners at Annapolis, Md., being sent away to Camp Chase, are passing by our quarters *en route* for there to-day.

June 21. A fine day. Don't feel well at all. Five men from out of our ward put in the dead house for punishment, for violating the rules of said hospital.

June 22. A fine day. Am rather on the decline of health to-day. A man by the name of Alexander Wallace died at half past 11 to-day from amputation of the left arm some days previously.

June 23. A fine day. Feel pretty well. Reported at headquarters (Dr. Bacon's office) and was examined by him; found unfit for duty, and told that I would not be fit, during my time, to return to my tent.

June 24. A fine day. Feel pretty well. They are burying Wallace to-day. Was presented with a very nice book by Mrs. Trall, of Connecticut, and Mrs. Bostwick. The Freemasons have a grand pic-nic in the grove close by.

June 25. A fine day. Feel pretty well. Went to the creek to bathe. Sent a card, given to me by a kind woman, whose name I have mislaid, to see if I could get a transfer to my own State.

June 26. A fine day; preaching in the grove; I feel much better to-day.

June 27. A fine day; went to the creek to bathe, it being two miles down and two miles back, making a walk of 4 miles.

June 28. A fine day. Turned over all our clothing to the ward-master, and am improving in health as fast as can be expected.

June 29. A very fine day, and a very nice place

here, making it pleasant to us sick and wounded soldiers.

June 30. A fine day. All exchanged prisoners mustered by the sergeant in charge of said hospital for pay and commutation of rations; being a prisoner for two hundred and twenty-four days, of course I was mustered with them.

July 1. A very warm day; showery all day. Nothing worthy of note in camp to-day.

July 2. A fine forenoon. Drew clothing at 12 o'clock; rained hard. Am not so well to-day.

July 3. A fine day; am very unwell to-day.

July 4. A fine day; at sun-rise two salutes were fired from the cannon, and at 11 o'clock we were marched down to the grove close by, and after prayer, a tune from the brass band, and then the Declaration of Independence was read by Dr. Bacon, surgeon in charge, and afterwards a splendid dinner. So ends the Fourth.

July 5. A fine day, and I enjoyed the Fourth very well; fire-lights were kept up till 11 o'clock at night, when I went to bed; on awakening I found myself pretty well.

July 6. A fine day; went to the river to bathe.

July 7. A fine day; went to the river to bathe. A report of the rebels advancing on this place. In tolerably good health.

July 8. A fine morning. One hundred and fifty wounded soldiers sent from Fredericksburg to Annapolis; the rebels on their retreat.

July 9. A fine day; gathered myself some dewberries, and went to the river to bathe.

July 10. A fine day, clear and warm. Great excitement for fear of the rebels entering this place.

July 11. A fine day. The excitement not so great to-day about the rebels invading Maryland.

July 12. A very nice day; not so well to-day. A man by the name of Steinseifer died in our ward at 11 o'clock.

July 13. A fine day. All the sick and wounded are in Annapolis, having had to skedaddle from Annapolis Junction on yesterday at 5 o'clock in the evening, on account of the rebels advancing on that place.

July 14. A fine day. At half past 3 o'clock got orders to return to Annapolis Junction; we arrived there at 5 o'clock in the evening, and found all as when we left it—being twenty miles down and twenty miles up again, making in all 40 miles.

July 15. A fine, clear day. A house burned down in sight of our quarters, thought to have taken fire from the soldiers of the 84th New York cooking in it.

July 16. A fine, clear day. Went out blackberrying, and took a walk to the grave-yard for the first time, to see where the soldiers were buried.

July 17. A very fine day. Picked a quart of blackberries. Preaching in the grove at 11 o'clock. Feel some better to-day

July 18. A fine, clear day. Got a transfer from the War Department to Philadelphia for medical treatment, and furnished with transportation to leave in the morning at 8 o'clock.

July 19. A fine day. Left Annapolis Junction and came to Baltimore, to South Gay street, No. 7. Got transportation from there to Philadelphia, making a distance of 98 miles.

July 20. A fine, clear day. Don't feel so well. Wrote a letter to Annapolis Junction to J. W. Powers and David Kautz. A man died in our ward at 4 o'clock.

July 21. A fine, clear day. Feel pretty well, and am improving as fast as can be expected. I am in a very nice hospital, and everything nice around us makes it very pleasant to us sick soldiers.

July 22. A fine day. A great fire in Philadelphia —the machine-shop for making government wagons burned to the ground.

July 23. A fine, pleasant day. Feel somewhat better to-day.

July 24. A fine, clear day. Went to preaching in the reading-room, or 19th ward, in the afternoon of this day, for the first time since I came here. This hospital is five miles out from the city of Philadelphia, on the Germantown road, on a high and elevated piece of ground—a very nicely got up building for this purpose, and said to have cost one hundred and fifty thousand dollars to build it.

July 25. Rained all night, and still raining this morning. Got a letter from home stating that my brother Joseph was in Philadelphia, in Broad and Cherry Hospital, badly wounded. The strangest occurrence was this: three years ago, he left three weeks before me for the army, he starting east and I starting also for the army, being sent west—and did not see each other for the space of three years—I having marched or traveled through Ohio, Indiana, Virginia, Kentucky, Tennessee, Alabama, Georgia, South Carolina, North Carolina, Virginia again, Maryland, and then into Pennsylvania, and passed within five miles of him, and then that we should meet each other; going away from home in good health, and now meeting again, not one able to walk or help the other, on account of his being wounded badly and my disease from the effects of imprisonment for two hundred and twenty-four days.

July 26. A fine day. Got a pass to go see brother Joseph at Philadelphia, and I can assure you it was a happy meeting to both of us, that we should be spared through the period of three years and through the battles and fiery trials that we had to pass through, and then be permitted to meet here and see each other once more.

July 27. A fine, clear day; don't feel well at all; bad pain in my head, and my feet swollen badly.

July 28. A very fine, pleasant day. Am very sick to-day.

July 29. A fine, clear day. No better yet; nothing worthy of note to-day.

July 30. A fine day. Not improving much in health, although the attendance given me is all that I could expect or wish for.

July 31. A fine, clear day. Feel some better; a great many visitors in and out to see us to-day.

Aug. 1. A fine, warm day, clear all through; feel middling well to-day.

Aug. 2. A warm forenoon, but rained hard in the afternoon.

Aug. 3. A fine forenoon. Got a pass in the afternoon to go to the city to see brother Joseph; went on the steam cars, as I was not able to walk—five miles down and five miles up again, making 10 miles.

Aug. 4. A wet, damp morning; don't feel well at all; my feet swollen badly and sharp pain in the head.

Aug. 5. A fine day; feel some better. Was presented with two nice books by a lady from Germantown.

Aug. 6. A fine, warm and clear day. Don't feel so well.

Aug. 7. A fine, clear day. Inspection of wards and patients; on night-watch for the first time at this place.

Aug. 8. A fine, clear day; am improving slowly in health. Got a very nice book presented to me by a gentleman from Germantown.

Aug. 9. A fine, warm, clear day. Got word in the evening from Joseph that he was worse, to come to the city to see him, which gave me much uneasiness of mind during the night.

Aug. 10. A fine, clear, warm day. Got a pass to the city to see brother Joseph, and found him very low indeed, and suffering badly from his wounds; stayed all day with him and returned in the evening, making a distance of 10 miles.

Aug. 11. A warm day. Received my descriptive-list from the captain of our company.

Aug. 12. A fine, clear day. Went to Capt. Kendall about my descriptive-list, that I returned to Doctor Curtis for him, he (Kendall) being in the city at the time.

Aug. 13. A fine day. The paymaster is here paying off those who have their descriptive-lists and signed the pay-roll since coming here.

Aug. 14. A fine day, exceedingly hot. Bad with neuralgia in my head.

Aug. 15. A fine day. Almost crazy with neuralgia in my head, don't feel near so well.

Aug. 16. A fine, clear day. Received ten dollars from home for Joseph and myself. Am very unwell to-day.

Aug. 17. A fine, warm day. Went to the city; gave Joseph seven dollars. Am a great deal better to-day.

Aug. 18. A fine day, and feel a great deal better. Presented with a very nice book.

Aug. 19. A fine, clear day, and am some better to-day.

Aug. 20. A fine, nice day, and feel a great deal better to-day.

Aug. 21. A fine, clear, warm day. Had a fight in our ward, the parties being a man of the 4th Ohio and a sergeant of our ward.

Aug. 22. A fine day. Helped to whitewash our ward. Feel a great deal better.

Aug. 23. A fine, clear day. Wrote a letter to Dr. Bacon, surgeon in charge of Annapolis Junction Hospital, concerning my pay for commutation of rations while a prisoner.

Aug. 24. A fine, nice, clear day. Went to the city to see Joseph—making a distance of 10 miles. In the evening received a letter from home with bad news in it of the death of my brother-in-law, William Myers, on the 20th of August, 1864.

Aug. 25. A fine, clear day. Feel pretty well. There was a prize of five hundred dollars on a ball-play between the Philadelphians and New Yorkers, the Philadelphians winning that sum.

Aug. 26. A fine, clear day. Don't feel so well.

Aug. 27. A fine, clear day. Received a letter from my captain, J. S. M'Bride, informing me of the members and company's health and welfare, and wishing me the return of good health and strength, giving his and their best respects and kindest wishes.

Aug. 28. A fine day, and very pleasant. Had inspection. Don't feel so well, with a bad cough, and a severe pain in my head.

Aug. 29. A fine day. Some twelve rebel prisoners brought to this hospital, wounded badly. Some of our men's time having expired, they were discharged and sent away.

Aug. 30. A fine, clear day. Feel some better.

Aug. 31. A fine, clear day. Was mustered by Lewis Taylor, sergeant in charge, for our pay. Many visitors in and out. Have charge of the dining room key for the evening, the cook having gone visiting.

Sept. 1. A fine, pleasant, cool day. Not well today; my feet swelled bad again and a severe pain in the head.

Sept. 2. A fine day. Went to the city to see my brother Joseph and found him in good spirits, and improving fast; returned in the evening, making a distance of 10 miles.

Sept. 3. A fine morning. Suffering a great deal from swollen feet and a severe pain in the head.

Sept. 4. A fine day. Sent for by Dr. Curtis, to report at his office, and after examination he presented me with a blank of recommendation for a discharge, to be filled up by Dr. E. Brown, surgeon of ward 5.

Sept. 5. A very wet, cool day. Dr. M. Norris filled out my blank for discharge, and returned it to sergeant Lewis Taylor, in charge of said hospital.

Sept. 6. A cool, wet morning. Wrote a letter to Col. Wm. Hoffman, Commissary-General of Prisoners of War, Washington, D. C.

Sept. 7. A fine day, and feel much better again to-day.

Sept. 8. A fine, cool day. Was transferred from ward 5 to ward 20, beat 72, at 1 o'clock of this day.

Sept. 9. A fine day. On guard, post No. 5. Feel pretty well. The first duty done by me since I was taken prisoner, and the first time that I am able to do it.

Sept. 10. A fine, clear day. Many patients coming into this hospital to-day from the front, and badly off.

Sept. 11. A very wet morning. Detailed on guard, No. 8 post. Examined by my doctor of ward in the morning, at noon by Dr. Curtis.

Sept. 12. A wet, cool day. Came off guard, and was examined by the Board, and pronounced unfit for duty. Went to the city, and returned at 8 in the evening—making a distance of ten miles.

Sept. 13. A fine, clear, cool day. Detailed for **outside** guard at this hospital.

Sept. 14. A fine, clear day. Came off guard, and was sent for to report to Lewis Curtis, executive officer, concerning my discharge. Received a visit from the Rev. J. B. Dales, of Philadelphia; he stating that the Rev. Mr. Wallace, of Westmoreland Co., Pa., requested him to visit me and my brother Joseph also, and if **we** were in need of any thing to add to our comfort or **welfare that they were ready to** furnish it for us. Thank God for them as friends, and not them alone, to console us in those hours of a **weak** and deranged system. Oh, how cheering to the heart to think of!

Sept. 15. A fine day. Detailed for **guard,** and feel pretty well to-day.

Sept. 16. A fine day. Came off guard, ward 9, post 6, having been guarding wounded rebel soldiers. Five months ago they were guarding me in Danville Hospital, I being very sick and a prisoner there; but I **suppose, as Paddy said when the log rolled over** him, I suppose time about is **fair play,** if it should be harder on the one side than the other.

Sept. 17. A fine day. On guard, post 11; came off at dark, on at 7 o'clock, and off again at 9 at night.

Sept. 18. A fine day. James Jeffries came to see **me, on a visit** from Irwin's Station.

Sept. 19. A fine day. Went to the city, making a **distance of 10 miles,** and met J. Jeffries in North Tenth street.

Sept. 20. A **fine** day. Detailed for guard at headquarters, post 8, this being my last day, my time having expired on this day, being three years and five days since our regiment was organized and sworn into service.

Sept. 21. A fine day. Came off guard. Went to see Dr. Curtis to let him know my time was out; he said he thought my papers had come, and that I would get them in a few days.

Sept. 22. A fine day. Had written a letter to Col. Hoffman. Went to the office in time to withdraw the letter, as he had sent me a certificate for the amount of seventy-three dollars and seventy-three cents due me from the government for rations while a prisoner in Richmond and Danville, Va.

Sept. 23. A fine, clear day. Got a pass to go to the city to draw the above named certificate. Went to No. 828 Walnut street, and was paid by Captain J. B. Wiggin, seventy-three dollars and seventy-three cents, being the full amount, and returned back, making 10 miles.

Sept. 24. A very wet day. Went to see Doctor Murphy about my discharge; he told me the papers had gone to Harrisburg, and as soon as they were returned I would get them, that they were all right.

Sept. 25. A fine, cool day. Inspected by Sergt. Lewis Taylor in the forenoon; in the afternoon J. Jeffries, and brother from Philadelphia, came to see me.

Sept. 26. A fine day. Received from my Captain J. S. M'Bride a certificate for the same amount as the one above collected, he not knowing I had already got it.

Sept. 27. A fine, clear day. Detailed for guard to fill a vacant post.

Sept. 28. A fine day. After dinner invited to attend a Bible class in the reading room, or ward 10, by a very nice woman giving me a card, showing the hours of meeting; a few minutes afterwards received my discharge from service, my time having expired.

Sept. 29. Left M'Clellan U. S. Hospital and came to the city of Philadelphia, 1230 Walnut street, and drew $300.63, and from there to Broad and Cherry Street Hospital, where I stayed all night with my brother Joseph, making a distance of 6 miles.

Sept. 30. A wet morning. Went to depot No. 1307 and 905 Walnut street; came back, got my dinner, and called on the sergeant in charge, but did not see him.

Oct. 1. A fine morning. Went to see Dr. Thomas Brainerd, in charge of Broad and Cherry Hospital, Phila., concerning Joseph's discharge, and he advised him to stay and get his papers and money before he would go home; he said that if I was satisfied he would let him go, but it would be his advice for him to stay. So on this night, at 10 o'clock I got transportation and returned home, arriving there on the 2d day of October, 1864, and joined my friends and little family, after an absence of three years and eighteen days in Uncle Sam's service; making a distance of three hundred and thirteen miles from Philadelphia to Turtle Creek, Pa., my place of starting and my home on my return.

Having finished these pages with these various items in them, and given you but very few of the incidents connected with my marchings of five thousand five hundred and eighty-five miles, I don't wish you to suppose that I have seen every thing—or that I have been in every battle during the war—or that I killed so-and-so many men while fighting—and that I have done this and that, as many of my fellow-soldiers have said on their return home to friends and relations; for I cannot say that I ever killed, or even disabled one man, during those three years and eighteen days in Uncle Sam's service, although many have been the well-aimed shots by me at the enemy. But how can I or any other man tell who or who did not cause any of his country's enemies to bite the dust, as thousands of muskets were fired off at the same time? for no one can speak fairly and not say, I cannot tell. My answer is, I cannot say that I ever did. I would simply say, that I have endeavored to fulfill my duty toward my country, in giving what little assistance I could in quelling the rebellion and having peace restored to our beloved country; nor do I think that anything has been left undone, so far as required of me and my physical strength and ability would allow me; as I can show vouchers that cannot be ruled out, and certificates that cannot be challenged, to that effect.

Finally, I wish to inform you that these pages were not filled up with the intention of being offered to the public, but for the information only of my little family, should I be spared to return to them again; and if well studied and reflected upon, they may be a school to the young and a lesson to the oldest and wisest of us.

A SONG

COMPOSED ON OUR ROAD TO KENTUCKY.

Six months and more after date,
A soldier's song I am going to relate;
Which happened on the sixteenth of September,
As one and all will remember.

Come all ye bold volunteers, come, listen to my rhyme,
The hardships of a soldier I now mean to explain;
All for the sake of the Union I left my friends so dear,
And enlisted in the army as a bold volunteer.

We left Monongahela City with hearts as stout as steel,
All for to meet the enemy upon the battle-field;
Our friends were on the river side, to wish us all good-bye,
You could see the tears falling from many a weeping eye.

Our conveyance was a steamboat that bore us from the shore,
To leave our native homes and friends perhaps to see no more,
In gliding down the river it filled our hearts with pride
To hear the cheers for Union a-roaring from each side.

They landed us in Pittsburgh, our quarters there were good;
They took us to the Girard House, and there we got our food.
The night being spent e'er the light it came again,
Then they marched us down to the cars when pouring down rain.

Then next upon the rail road they hurried us by steam,
The people from the country all along the road did team;
One cheer was heard all along the line;
I never have witnessed such an exciting time.

Altoona was our dining place, and it was nearly night,
But when we can to Huntingdon it filled us with delight;
The ladies of that little place, with hearts both stout and brave,
And when the engine started their handkerchiefs did wave.

We landed in Lancaster, and they marched us up through town,
And in a hook and ladder house we had to lie down;
With neither bed nor blanket we lay to take our rest,
And meditate upon our friends whom we left in distress.

They marched us on to Harrisburg, and ordered us to stay
Until we were disciplined, that we might march away;
It was then I just began to know what it was to be in want,
And the hardships of a soldier when he is in camp.

We quartered in a swamp, our bed was straw and hay,
We took it without quarreling, and down our heroes lay;
Our rations were dealt out, of bread and meat likewise,
I thought I saw starvation staring in our eyes.

Four pounds of bread for six of us was scarcely enough for three,
But still we stand the hardships all for our country;
Her laws and constitution for ever we'll maintain,
And against our old Uncle Sam we never will complain.

Oh, now I'm going to conclude and finish up my song,
The truth I have explained to you as far as I have gone.
May God protect our army, and guide them in the field,
In conquering our enemy in the battle and make them yield.

ADAM S. JOHNSTON.

www.ingramcontent.com/pod-product-compliance
Lightning Source LLC
Chambersburg PA
CBHW022132160426
43197CB00009B/1251